Praise for Stephen

"A poet who time and again achieves th[...] ordinary. [Stephen Dunn] can take you by the hand and lead you along a street you may have passed through every day without much notice, and suddenly, at this new angle, the ordinary reveals in itself all the splendor and terror of existence."

—Rita Dove, *Washington Post*

"The art lies in hiding the art, Horace tells us, and Stephen Dunn has proven himself a master of concealment. His honesty would not be so forceful were it not for his discrete formality; his poems would not be so strikingly naked were they not so carefully dressed."

—Billy Collins

"Stephen Dunn has a gift for aphorism, but his most startling ability is the way he maps out the subtle, mordant shifts of adult morality."

—*New York Times Book Review*

"Dunn's poetry is the poetry of experience, of humor, of irony, of daily life, of love—and of the most elegant verbal sparring with the self."

—Alicia Ostriker

"There's a deep and reliable honesty that drives [Dunn's] poems. . . . That the poems manage this kind of transmission of (no other word for it) truth, and make that truth so much a delight to hear—well, that's what Stephen Dunn has been doing all his writing life. That's why his poems have been, and remain, indispensable."

—Robert Wrigley

CHAPBOOKS

Keeper of Limits: The Mrs. Cavendish Poems
Falling Backwards into the World
Winter at the Caspian Sea (with Lawrence Raab)
Five Impersonations

BOOKS ABOUT STEPHEN DUNN

The Room and the World: Essays on the Poet Stephen Dunn
(edited by Laura McCullough)

The

NOT YET

FALLEN

WORLD

New and Selected Poems

STEPHEN DUNN

W. W. NORTON & COMPANY
Independent Publishers Since 1923

For information about permission to reproduce selections from this book, write to
Permissions, W. W. Norton & Company, Inc., 500 Fifth Avenue, New York, NY 10110

For information about special discounts for bulk purchases, please contact
W. W. Norton Special Sales at specialsales@wwnorton.com or 800-233-4830

Manufacturing by Lakeside Book Company
Production manager: Beth Steidle

Library of Congress Cataloging-in-Publication Data

Names: Dunn, Stephen, date–date, author.
Title: The not yet fallen world : new and selected poems / Stephen Dunn.
Description: First edition. | New York, NY : W. W. Norton & Company, 2022. |
Includes index.
Identifiers: LCCN 2021061124 | ISBN 9780393882254 (hardcover) |
ISBN 9780393882261 (epub)
Subjects: LCGFT: Poetry.
Classification: LCC PS3554.U49 N68 2022 | DDC 811/.54—dc23/eng/20211217
LC record available at https://lccn.loc.gov/2021061124

ISBN 978-1-324-07466-3 pbk.

W. W. Norton & Company, Inc., 500 Fifth Avenue, New York, N.Y. 10110
www.wwnorton.com

W. W. Norton & Company Ltd., 15 Carlisle Street, London W1D 3BS

1 2 3 4 5 6 7 8 9 0

My gratitude and love to my wife Barbara Hurd for her generosity of spirit and critical acumen, and to my children Andrea and Susanne, and to their mother, so important in my early years. And to my devoted and insightful readers Sam Toperoff, BJ Ward, Jill Rosser, and especially to Lawrence Raab, without whom as friend and critic I couldn't have made it this far.

ACKNOWLEDGMENTS

The poems in this volume were not chosen to suggest a chronology, rather a series of interests and concerns. —S.D.

•

Most of these poems are from the following collections published by W. W. Norton:

Pagan Virtues
Whereas
Lines of Defense
Here and Now
What Goes On: Selected and New Poems 1995–2009
Everything Else in the World
The Insistence of Beauty
Local Visitations
Different Hours
Loosestrife
New and Selected Poems: 1974–1994
Landscape at the End of the Century
Between Angels

•

Poems first published in *Local Time* (William Morrow); in *Not Dancing*, *Work and Love*, *A Circus of Needs*, and *Full of Lust and Good Usage* (all from Carnegie-Mellon University Press); and in *Looking for Holes in the Ceiling* (University of Massachusetts Press) appear in the versions reprinted in *New and Selected Poems: 1974–1994* (W. W. Norton). "Elementary" (from *Work and Love*) and "From Underneath" (from *Local Time*) were not included in *New and Selected Poems*.

Nine new poems are included here, the first four having appeared in
The James Dickey Review:

"The Prayer You Asked For"
"In the Battle Against Tyranny"
"Love Poem Near the End of the World"
"During the Pandemic"
"Fascinations"
"Becoming Oneself"
"Before the Storm"
"The 6:10 to Happiness"
"The Color of Nightfall"

•

"The Vanishings" was selected by Louise Glück for
The Best American Poetry 1995.

"Five Roses in the Morning" was selected by Paul Muldoon for
The Best American Poetry 2005.

"Where He Found Himself" was selected by Heather McHugh for
The Best American Poetry 2007.

"The Imagined" was selected by Mark Doty for
The Best American Poetry 2013.

Loosestrife was a finalist for the
National Book Critics Circle Award in 1996.

Different Hours was awarded the Pulitzer Prize in 2001.

CONTENTS

The

NOT YET

FALLEN

WORLD

1

PROPOSITIONS

What does a pig know about bacon?
—RANDALL JARRELL

Anyone who begins a sentence with, "In all honesty . . ."
is about to tell a lie. Anyone who says, "This is how I feel"
had better love form more than disclosure. Same for anyone
who thinks he thinks well because he had a thought.

If you say, "You're ugly" to an ugly person—no credit
for honesty, which must always be a discovery, an act
that qualifies as an achievement. If you persist
you're just a cruel bastard, a pig without a mirror,

somebody who hasn't examined himself enough.
A hesitation hints at an attempt to be honest, suggests
a difficulty is present. A good sentence needs
a clause or two, interruptions, set off by commas,

evidence of a slowing down, a rethinking.
Before I asked my wife to marry me, I told her
I'd never be fully honest. No one, she said,
had ever said that to her. I was trying

to be radically honest, I said, but in fact
had another motive. A claim without a "but" in it
is, at best, only half true. In all honesty,
I was asking in advance to be forgiven.

3

TRAVELING
(FROM "SYMPATHETIC MAGIC")

If you travel alone, hitchhiking,
sleeping in woods,
make a cathedral of the moonlight
that reaches you, and lie down in it.
Shake a box of nails
at the night sounds
for there is comfort in your own noise.
And say out loud:
somebody at sunrise be distraught
for love of me,
somebody at sunset call my name.
There will soon be company.
But if the moon clouds over
you have to live with disapproval.
You are a traveler,
you know the open, hostile smiles
of those stuck in their lives.
Make a fire.
If the Devil sits down, offering companionship,
tell him you've always admired
his magnificent, false moves.
Then recite the list
of what you've learned to do without.
It is stronger than prayer.

HISTORY

It's like this, the king marries
a commoner, and the populace cheers.
She doesn't even know how to curtsy,
but he loves her manners in bed.
Why doesn't he do what his father did,
the king's mother wonders—
those peasant girls brought in
through that secret entrance, that's how
a kingdom works best. But marriage!
The king's mother won't come out
of her room, and a strange democracy
radiates throughout the land,
which causes widespread dreaming,
a general hopefulness. This is,
of course, how people get hurt,
how history gets its ziggy shape.
The king locks his wife in the tower
because she's begun to ride
her horse far into the woods.
How unqueenly to come back
to the castle like that,
so sweaty and flushed. The only answer,
his mother decides, is stricter rules—
no whispering in the corridors,
no gaiety in the fields.
The king announces his wife is very tired
and has decided to lie down,
and issues an edict that all things yours
are once again his.
This is the kind of law
history loves, that contains
its own demise. The villagers conspire

for years, waiting for the right time,
which never arrives. There's only
that one person, not exactly brave,
but too unhappy to be reasonable,
who crosses the moat, scales the walls.

ELEMENTARY

1

There was death.
And there was the occasional touching
which reminded the body
it was alone.
And there was the weeping.
And the laughter which understood death.
And the laughter we couldn't bear.

2

There was the house or the apartment.
And there was the office
or the factory or the field.
And there was sleep.
And there was the in between.
If work was satisfying
love was possible.
If we loved power there was
an emptiness that never stopped
needing to be filled.

3

There was fire, water, air,
and machines that made them ours.
There were wild things
and things on shelves.
And there was boredom when the rain fell,
boredom on the most beautiful days.

After the pleasures came
we wanted them to return.
And got sad.

4

There was play, our bodies in motion
forgetting they would die.
And the sudden remembering
after the sweat dried.
And there were the questions,
the old ones, over and over.
And the hard work in the yard,
the routine erasures,
the cleansing of hands.

5

There was language.
And what had to be written
because it couldn't be said.
And there were the translations
from other languages.
And the daily translations
of our own.
And each thing in the world
had a name,
and was waiting for a name.
And there was silence
with its history of bad timing
coming our way again.

TUCSON

A man was dancing with the wrong woman
in the wrong bar, the wrong part of town.
He must have chosen the woman, the place,
as keenly as you choose what to wear
when you dress to kill.
And the woman, who could have said no,
must have made her choice years ago,
to look like the kind of trouble
certain men choose as their own.
I was there for no good reason myself,
with a friend looking for a friend,
but I'm not important.
They were dancing close
when a man from the bar decided
the dancing was wrong. I'd forgotten
how fragile the face is, how fists too
are just so many small bones.
The bouncer waited, then broke in.
Someone wiped up the blood.
The woman began to dance
with another woman, each in tight jeans.
The air pulsed. My hands
were fidgety, damp.
We were Mexicans, Indians, whites.
The woman was part this, part that.
My friend said nothing's wrong, stay put,
it's a good fighting bar, you won't get hurt
unless you need to get hurt.

IF A CLOWN

If a clown came out of the woods,
a standard-looking clown with oversized
polka-dot clothes, floppy shoes,
a red, bulbous nose, and you saw him
on the edge of your property,
there'd be nothing funny about that,
would there? A bear might be preferable,
especially if black and berry-driven.
And if this clown began waving his hands
with those big, white gloves
that clowns wear, and you realized
he wanted your attention, had something
apparently urgent to tell you,
would you pivot and run from him,
or stay put, as my friend did, who seemed
to understand here was a clown
who didn't know where he was,
a clown without context.
What could be sadder, my friend thought,
than a clown in need of a context?
If then the clown said to you
that he was on his way to a kid's
birthday party, his car had broken down,
and he needed a ride, would you give
him one? Or would the connection
between the comic and the appalling,
as it pertained to clowns, be suddenly so clear
that you'd be paralyzed by it?
And if you were the clown, and my friend
hesitated, as he did, would you make
a sad face, and with an enormous finger
wipe away an imaginary tear? How far

would you trust your art? I can tell you
it worked. Most of the guests had gone
when my friend and the clown drove up,
and the family was angry. But the clown
twisted a balloon into the shape of a bird
and gave it to the kid, who smiled,
let it rise to the ceiling. If you were the kid,
the birthday boy, what from then on
would be your relationship with disappointment?
With joy? Whom would you blame or extol?

Because in large cities the famous truths
already had been plumbed and debated,
the metaphysicians of South Jersey lowered
their gaze, just tried to be themselves.
They'd gather at coffee shops in Vineland
and deserted shacks deep in the Pine Barrens.
Nothing they came up with mattered
so they were free to be eclectic, and as odd
as getting to the heart of things demanded.
They walked undisguised on the boardwalk.
At the Hamilton Mall they blended
with the bargain-hunters and the feckless.
Almost everything amazed them,
the last hour of a county fair,
blueberry fields covered with mist.
They sought the approximate weight of sadness,
its measure and coloration. But they liked
a good ball game too, well pitched, lots of zeroes
on the scoreboard. At night when they lay down,
exhausted and enthralled, their spouses knew
it was too soon to ask any hard questions.
Come breakfast, as always, the metaphysicians
would begin to list the many small things
they'd observed and thought, unable to stop talking
about this place and what a world it was.

THE STORYTELLER

God was listening, but even so
    I never told the truth
in confession. If I'd stolen candy

from Woolworths, I'd say I took
    the Lord's name
in vain eleven times, Father,

since my last confession. If I'd
    been good,
I'd say I took the Lord's name

six or seven times. I knew the priest
    depended on sins
to feel good about his job,

but most of all I wanted to get back
    to the religion
of the schoolyard as fast as possible,

to epiphanous spin moves off the post
    and soft reverse layups.
Thus I never properly did penance

at the altar, two Hail Mary's
    instead of four,
a fast Our Father, maybe half

an Act of Contrition or Apostles'
    Creed.
I don't know why I never was afraid

of God and his famous penchant
    for punishment.
I don't know why Hell

didn't scare me, why it seemed
    like some movie
with special effects. Angels, though,

were real, like invisible friends
    you could count on.
I remember thinking angels could make

a shot go in, angels were what prayers
    were all about.
When my friend Brian said

he was going to confess to Father Kelly
    that he masturbated,
I told him look, no, don't stir up

Father Kelly, tell him you took
    the Lord's name in vain
three hundred times and were very sorry,

but Brian said God was listening,
    God *knew*,
and anyway, he would be forgiven,

that was the thing about being Catholic,
    stupid, your sins
could be forgiven. I knew he was right,

but I went right on confessing
    to Jesus Christs,
goddamns, Christs Almighty, words

I never in fact said, but words I knew
        were the right words
for the occasion.

She taught theater, so we gathered
in the theater.
We praised her voice, her knowledge,
how good she was
with *Godot* and just four months later
with *Gigi*.
She was fifty. The problem in the liver.
Each of us recalled
an incident in which she'd been kind
or witty.
I told about being unable to speak
from my diaphragm
and how she made me lie down, placed her hand
where the failure was
and showed me how to breathe.
But afterwards
I only could do it when I lay down
and that became a joke
between us, and I told it as my offering
to the audience.
I was on stage and I heard myself
wishing to be impressive.
Someone else spoke of her cats
and no one spoke
of her face or the last few parties.
The fact was
I had avoided her for months.

It was a student's turn to speak, a sophomore,
one of her actors.
She was a drunk, he said, often came to class
reeking.

Sometimes he couldn't look at her, the blotches,
the awful puffiness.
And yet she was a great teacher,
he loved her,
but thought someone should say
what everyone knew
because she didn't die by accident.

Everyone was crying. Everyone was crying and it
was almost over now.
The remaining speaker, an historian, said he'd cut
his speech short.
And the Chairman stood up as if by habit,
said something about loss
and thanked us for coming. None of us moved
except some students
to the student who'd spoken, and then others
moved to him, across dividers,
down aisles, to his side of the stage.

2

ROUND TRIP

I

I watched the prairie repeat itself
    until it got beautiful, the geometry
        of farms, the flatness

that made interesting the slightest
    undulation. Never had the sky
        touched so far down.

Then, because mood invents landscape,
    the flatness turned irredeemable,
        I felt it go on and on—

something lush and vacant in me
    wished for an edge again,
        a city, an ocean.

I returned east, began to revise
    my childhood, wanted women
        with sharp tongues,

my evening walks shadowy and open
    to possibility. And because the mind
        gets what it wants

but rarely the way it wants it,
    I got mugged on a street corner,
        fear brought home in a real cold sweat

on a real November evening,
   and city life began to insist—
      like jazz, like dream—

it would be nothing but what it was.
   In a rented cabin up north,
      Christmas vacation,

I closed the door and gave whatever in me
   wanted to be alone and pitied
      its hard uncomfortable chair.

But after a while the light
   I didn't believe in
      shone in anyway through the windows,

the walls I had pulled in
   closer and closer
      returned to their proper places.

One day I opened the door
   and it wasn't quite overcast,
      little pieces of sun

reached the tip of my shoe,
   and it was as if I'd touched a breast
      for the first time

and touched it and touched it
   until, having touched it enough,
      I finally saw the blue veins . . .

Ever since, I've been trying to build
a house of cards amid a house
    of people, hard edges and angles,

each one overlapping. From the beginning
I've been careful of the one
    that would be too many.

I've kept out of drafts, house-winds.
The unexpected opening
    of a door, an indelicate voice,

these are the hazards of building
amid people, amid their enthusiasms
    and secret needs

to destroy. One should be alone
to build a house of cards.
    One should have a hardwood table,

perfectly flat. One should have none
of the clutter that comes
    from living a life.

That's why, though, I've been trying
to build a house of cards
    in a house of people—

to do what's difficult to do
and so be pleased
    with each card I add,

each moment short of collapse.

There's been a cricket in the living room,
    a male because only the male
        is built to sing

or to produce what passes for song.
    It's a mating call, that high sound
        that comes from rubbing

forewing against forewing, plaintive,
    like someone scared blowing
        a little whistle in the dark.

Day and night it's been making that sound
    from somewhere in the room.
    I've opened drawers,

I've pulled chairs away from the wall,
    ready with two paper cups
        to catch it

and take it outside. It came in, I suppose,
    in a confusion of warmth,
        doomed to sing

its song to those who wouldn't understand.
    Now the song grows
        more faint—

why care? it's the end of summer
    and crickets die and come back
        in great, anonymous force.

I'm pulling back the rug, listening
　　for what it withholds
　　　　when anyone gets close.

4

Where does the dark come from?
—The dark comes from the weakness
of the infinity of numbers.

　　　　—ANDREA DUNN, AGE 10

How to leave and come back—the school bus
　　instructs my daughter it's easy
　　　　and that for now is good.

She's off again into numbers, words,
　　all the necessary confusions.
　　　　History, she believes,

is what happens to others. Biology is what
　　she lives with, but hasn't had.
　　　　I'm watching from the window,

the father who knows education
　　is all about departures, who knows
　　　　when things are right

nobody comes home the same. The school bus
　　has left a hole in the landscape.
　　　　Air fills it now, the low sky

we don't call sky for some reason.
　　How to paint a landscape where children
　　　　once played? Swirls and smudges?

My daughter knows where the dark comes from
and I believe her. She's growing breasts.
        She closes the door to her room.

I'd paint the trees blue because the low sky
        is in them. I'd paint the area white
            where she once did a cartwheel,

maybe with a hint of yellow in it
        for the school bus. Off to the side
            lots of red seemingly out of control

yet orderly, like wildflowers.

        5

Nothing's happening but the wind,
        the ferry rocking its way
            toward Delaware, and Delaware Bay

full of big tankers
        at anchor, seemingly poised.
            It's two hours across,

a talk to give, one night
        away, then two hours back,
            the kind of minor traveling

which tests nothing at home, nothing in self.
        "Travel is the saddest pleasure,"
            a friend once said. He meant

all those hours that exist
        outside of work and play and love.
            The boredom of sailors

must be enormous, as great as the boredom
   of those on land who hope for weather
      to change their lives.

We're bored too, the few of us
   making this trip, off-season, the specter
      of necessity

evident in how we sit and stare.
   Later, I'm thinking, each of us
      will have a story to tell

about the bay and the ships.
   We'll leave out all we can,
      all that is a traveler's life

or a sailor's life. We'll make our friends
   wish they were us, we'll replace experience
      with what we say.

   6

This is one of those stories,
   Minnesota to New Jersey,
      a return home

in search of home, regular departures
   to find the limits
      of home—

impulses finding reasons, words.

The great decisions that change
   a life—hardly decisions
      at all; a wild hunch

or avoidance, the unknown agent x
     coursing through the body
          like a bastard gene.

I'm only sure that collapse
     waits just beyond
          standing still,

the next complacency. Even now,
     my day off, I'm thinking
          I'll get in my car,

get out of here, no rhyme except
     internal rhyme, the clicks
          and bells that go off

when the body has heard itself
     and acted. I know where
          I'll go—

ball field, casino, deserted beach—
     some not-home place
          where I can pivot

at supper time, make my way back
     as if I'd made a choice.

7

Last week at this time
     Canada geese flapping overhead,
          heading south:

impossible to warn them of hunters
up since dawn. A few hours later
three separate phone calls

told me the same person was dead.
By the third my voice
had nothing in it;

it was days before the letting go.
I watched the jays in the yard
chasing smaller birds,

taking all the seed for themselves. That's where
the dark comes from, I thought,
some weakness in the motive

or of the heart, a bunch of jays
exercising their muscle, and *poof,*
nothing's left but jays.

I should have called the dead man's wife.
I should have reread his poems,
made him a good ghost

and myself sorrow's perfectly correct man.
I put on my running shoes,
ran the full circle

of the park, showered, turned on the
important game. The whole season
was on the line,

the announcer said, and it was.
In a nearby room the noise of others—
a child's whine, my wife saying No—

mixed with my noise to form
the familiar. For a while
nothing tumbled down.

3

ODYSSEUS'S SECRET

At first he thought only of home, and Penelope.
But after a few years, like anyone on his own,
he couldn't separate what he'd chosen
from what had chosen him. Calypso,
                    the Lotus-eaters, Circe;
a man could forget where he lived.
He had a gift for getting in and out of trouble,
a prodigious, human gift. To survive Cyclops
and withstand the Sirens' song—
just those words *survive, withstand,*
                    in his mind became a music
he moved to and lived by.
How could *govern,* even *love,* compete?
They belonged to a different part of a man,
the untested part, which never had transcended dread,
or the liar part, which always spoke like a citizen.
                    The larger the man, though,
the more he needed to be reminded
he was a man. Lightning, high winds;
for every excess a punishment.
Penelope *was* dear to him,
                    full of character and fine in bed.
But by the middle years this other life
had become his life. That was Odysseus's secret,
kept even from himself. When he talked about return
he thought he meant what he said.
                    Twenty years to get home?
A man finds his shipwrecks,
tells himself the necessary stories.
Whatever gods are—our own fearful voices
or intimations from the unseen order

of things, the gods finally released him,
               cleared the way.
Odysseus boarded that Phaeacian ship, suddenly tired
of the road's dangerous enchantments,
and sailed through storm and wild sea
as if his beloved were all that ever mattered.

WILD

The year I owned a motorcycle and split the air
in southern Spain, and could smell the oranges
in the orange groves as I passed them
outside of Seville, I understood
I'd been riding too long in cars,
probably even should get a horse,
become a high-up, flesh-connected thing
among the bulls and cows.
My brand-new wife had a spirit
that worried and excited me, a history
of moving on. Wine from a spigot for pennies,
langostinas and angulas, even the language
felt dangerous in my mouth. Mornings,
our icebox bereft of ice,
I'd speed on my motorcycle to the iceman's house,
strap a big rectangular block
to the extended seat where my wife often sat
hot behind me, arms around my waist.
In the streets the smell of olive oil,
the noise of men torn between church
and sex, their bodies taut, heretical.
And the women, buttoned-up,
or careless, full of public joy, a Jesus
around their necks.
Our neighbors showed us how to shut down
in the afternoon,
the stupidity of not respecting the sun.
They forgave us who we were.
Evenings we'd take turns with the Herald Tribune
killing mosquitoes, our bedroom walls bloody
in this country known for blood;
we couldn't kill enough.

When the Levante, the big wind, came out of Africa
with its sand and heat, disturbing things,
it brought with it a lesson, unlearnable,
of how far a certain wildness can go.
Our money ran out. I sold the motorcycle.
We moved without knowing it
to take our quieter places in the world.

AT THE SMITHVILLE METHODIST CHURCH

It was supposed to be Arts & Crafts for a week,
but when she came home
with the "Jesus Saves" button, we knew what art
was up, what ancient craft.

She liked her little friends. She liked the songs
they sang when they weren't
twisting and folding paper into dolls.
What could be so bad?

Jesus had been a good man, and putting faith
in good men was what
we had to do to stay this side of cynicism,
that other sadness.

O.K., we said. One week. But when she came home
singing "Jesus loves me,
the Bible tells me so," it was time to talk.
Could we say Jesus

doesn't love you? Could I tell her the Bible
is a great book certain people use
to make you feel bad? We sent her back
without a word.

It had been so long since we believed, so long
since we needed Jesus
as our nemesis and friend, that we thought he was
sufficiently dead,

that our children would think of him like Lincoln
or Thomas Jefferson.
Soon it became clear to us: you can't teach disbelief
to a child,

only wonderful stories, and we hadn't a story
nearly as good.
On parents' night there were the Arts & Crafts
all spread out

like appetizers. Then we took our seats
in the church
and the children sang a song about the Ark,
and Hallelujah

and one in which they had to jump up and down
for Jesus.
I can't remember ever feeling so uncertain
about what's comic, what's serious.

Evolution is magical but devoid of heroes.
You can't say to your child
"Evolution loves you." The story stinks
of extinction and nothing

exciting happens for centuries. I didn't have
a wonderful story for my child
and she was beaming. All the way home in the car
she sang the songs,

occasionally standing up for Jesus.
There was nothing to do
but drive, ride it out, sing along
in silence.

THE SACRED

After the teacher asked if anyone had
   a sacred place
and the students fidgeted and shrank

in their chairs, the most serious of them all
   said it was his car,
being in it alone, his tape deck playing

things he'd chosen, and others knew the truth
   had been spoken
and began speaking about their rooms,

their hiding places, but the car kept coming up,
   the car in motion,
music filling it, and sometimes one other person

who understood the bright altar of the dashboard
   and how far away
a car could take him from the need

to speak, or to answer, the key
   in having a key
and putting it in, and going.

THE DEATH OF GOD

When the news filtered to the angels
they were overwhelmed by their sudden aloneness.
Long into the night they waited for instructions;
the night was quieter than any night they'd known.
I don't have a thought in my head, one angel lamented.
Others worried, Is there such a thing as an angel now?
New to questioning, dashed by the dry light
of reason, some fell into despair. Many disappeared.
A few wandered naturally toward power, were hired
by dictators who needed something like an angel
to represent them to the world.
These angels spoke the pure secular word.
They murdered sweetly and extolled the greater good.
The Dark Angel himself was simply amused.

The void grew, and was fabulously filled.
Vast stadiums and elaborate malls—
the new cathedrals—were built
where people cheered and consumed.
At the nostalgia shops angel trinkets
and plastic crucifixes lined the shelves.
The old churches were homes for the poor.

And yet before meals and at bedtime
and in the iconographies of dreams,
God took his invisible place in the kingdom of need.
Disaffected minstrels made and sang His songs.
The angels were given breath and brain.
This all went on while He was dead to the world.

The Dark Angel observed it, waiting as ever.
On these things his entire existence depended.

THE PRAYER YOU ASKED FOR

For Carolyn, my sister-in-law

When I asked what you wanted for Christmas,
you said you wanted from me a prayer,
sincere, unironic, because you were
about to have surgery, and needed one.

I hereby pray that all goes well, and you heal
speedily and fully, and that the God
you believe in, a God of beneficence
and salvation, is listening.

Because you know I've long maintained
that to pray is to address a better part
of oneself, I want you to trust
that belief doesn't matter to me now,

only love does in this grand unruly scheme
of our lives together. And if there is
a celestial being, a possibility
for your sake I'll allow myself to entertain,

let Him descend as quietly and as invisibly
as ever. The only proof I want is your health,
some proper restoration of your body,
this Christmas and for years to come. Amen.

The woman with five hearts knew what she had,
knew what we lacked. She bet high and then
higher; it was what any of us would have done.
                    A woman with five hearts,
we concluded, was a dangerous thing.
She did not think it romantic, what she had.

    She knew it was better
than two pair, better than anything straight.
She was sure I, for example, had weakness,
three of something, at best.
                        The man to my right
clearly resented the woman with five hearts.
He touched her arm, as if this were a different game.
He tried to be ironic, but instead was mean.

    The woman with five hearts saw him
as a man with clubs, one fewer than he needed.
A man without enough clubs can be a pathetic thing.
Each of her bets demanded he come clean.
                        It was simple prudence
to yield to such a woman, a woman with all that.
The rest of us did, understanding so many hearts
could not be beaten, not with what we had.
But the man to my right decided to bluff.

    He raised her with what seemed
his entire body, everything he had been and was.
The woman with five hearts raised back,
amused now, as if aware of an old act—
            a man with nothing puffing himself up.
He stayed because by now it had all gone
too far, a woman with five hearts and a man
                        without enough clubs.
And when she showed him all five, beautifully red,
he had to admit that was exactly what she had.

THOSE OF US WHO THINK WE KNOW

Those of us who think we know
the same secrets
are silent together most of the time,
for us there is eloquence
in desire, and for a while
when in love and exhausted
it's enough to nod like shy horses
and come together
in a quiet ceremony of tongues.

It's in disappointment we look for words
to convince us
the spaces between stars are nothing
to worry about,
it's when those secrets burst
in that emptiness between our hearts
and the lumps in our throats.
And the words we find
are always insufficient, like love,
though they are often lovely
and all we have.

THE REVERSE SIDE

The reverse side also has a reverse side.
—JAPANESE PROVERB

It's why when we speak a truth
some of us instantly feel foolish
as if a deck inside us has been shuffled
and there it is—the opposite
of what we said.

And perhaps why as we fall in love
we're already falling out of it.

It's why the terrified and the simple
latch onto one story,
just one version of the great mystery.

Image & afterimage, oh even
the open-minded yearn for a fiction
to rein things in—
the snapshot, the lie of the frame.

How do we not go crazy,
we who have found ourselves compelled
to live with the circle, the ellipsis, the word
not yet written.

THE REVOLT OF THE TURTLES

On gray forgetful mornings like this
sea turtles would gather in the shallow waters
of the Gulf to discuss issues of self-presentation
and related concerns like, If there were a God
would he have a hard shell and a retractable head,
and whether speed on land
was of any importance to a good swimmer.

They knew that tourists needed to placate
their children with catchy stories, and amuse
themselves with various cruelties
such as turning turtles over on their backs
and watching their legs wriggle.
So the turtles formed a committee to address

How to Live Among People Who Among
Other Atrocities Want to Turn You into Soup.

The committee was also charged with wondering
if God would mind a retelling of their lives,
one in which sea turtles
were responsible for all things
right-minded and progressive, and men
and women for poisoning the water.

The oldest sea turtle among them knew
that whoever was in control of the stories
controlled all the shoulds and should-nots.
But he wasn't interested in punishment,
only ways in which power could bring about

fairness and decency. And when he finished speaking
in the now memorable and ever deepening

waters of the Gulf, all the sea turtles
began to chant Only Fairness, Only Decency.

TO A TERRORIST (1993)

For the historical ache, the ache passed down
which finds its circumstance and becomes
the present ache, I offer this poem

without hope, knowing there's nothing,
not even revenge, which alleviates
a life like yours. I offer it as one

might offer his father's ashes
to the wind, a gesture
when there's nothing else to do.

Still, I must say to you:
I hate your good reasons.
I hate the hatefulness that makes you fall

in love with death, your own included.
Perhaps you're hating me now,
I who own my own house

and live in a country so muscular,
so smug, it thinks its terror is meant
only to mean well, and to protect.

Christ turned his singular cheek,
one man's holiness another's absurdity.
Like you, the rest of us obey the sting,

the surge. I'm just speaking out loud
to cancel my silence. Consider it an old impulse,
doomed to become mere words.

The first poet probably spoke to thunder
and, for a while, believed
thunder had an ear and a choice.

IN THE BATTLE AGAINST TYRANNY

In the battle against tyranny
be prepared to lose a skirmish
or two. Maybe even more.
We need to know those in power
never forget people like us
have a score to settle, remain
galvanized by grief and rage.
They hire henchmen
so they can take naps
in the afternoon, and offset
the worry of enemies skulking
on the outskirts
of their enormous properties.
They want to be free to dream
of winding tunnels and fortified
stairways leading to places
where they can't be found.
But we the aggrieved always
have a sense of where they are.
It may take years before we find
the words that turn into a plan.
That's when we have to keep
hitting them hard above the belt.
Even after they catch on,
they're often fooled by tactics
not theirs. Remember
we have language now.
We can use it like a shield
to protect us
or to confuse them
with pretty stories
of ascensions into the clouds,

the ones in which kings
try to become gods, and discover
how sad it can be to succeed.

4

TIGER FACE

Because you can be what you're not
     for only so long,
one day the tiger cub raised by goats

wandered to the lake and saw himself.
     It was astounding
to have a face like that, cat-handsome,

hornless, and we can imagine he stared
     a long time, then sipped
and pivoted, bemused yet burdened now

with choice. The mother goat had nursed him.
     The others had tolerated
his silly quickness and claws.

And because once you know who you are
     you need not rush,
and good parents are a blessing

whoever they are, he went back to them,
     rubbing up against
their bony shins, keeping his secret to himself.

But after a while the tiger who'd found
     his true face
felt the disturbing hungers, those desires

to get low in the reeds, swish his tail,
     charge.
Because he was a cat he disappeared

without goodbyes, his goat-parents relieved
  such a thing was gone.

And we can imagine how, alone and beyond

choice, he wholly became who he was—
  that zebra or gazelle
stirring the great blood rush and odd calm

as he discovered, while moving, what needed
  to be done.

It was bring-your-own if you wanted anything
hard, so I brought Johnnie Walker Red
along with some resentment I'd held in
for a few weeks, which was not helped
by the sight of little nameless things
pierced with toothpicks on the tables,
or by talk that promised to be nothing
if not small. But I'd consented to come,
and I knew in what part of the house
their animals would be sequestered,
whose company I loved. What else can I say,

except that old retainer of slights and wrongs,
that bad boy I hadn't quite outgrown—
I'd brought him along, too. I was out
to cultivate a mood. My hosts greeted me,
but did not ask about my soul, which was when
I was invited by Johnnie Walker Red
to find the right kind of glass, and pour.
I toasted the air. I said hello to the wall,
then walked past a group of women
dressed to be seen, undressing them
one by one, and went up the stairs to where

the Rottweilers were, Rosie and Tom,
and got down with them on all fours.
They licked the face I offered them,
and I proceeded to slick back my hair
with their saliva, and before long
I felt like a wild thing, ready to mess up
the party, scarf the hors d'oeuvres.
But the dogs said, No, don't do that,

calm down, after a while they open the door
and let you out, they pet your head, and everything
you might have held against them is gone,
and you're good friends again. Stay, they said.

Last night Joan Sutherland was nuancing
the stratosphere on my fine-tuned tape deck,
and there was my dog Buster with a flea rash,
his head in his privates. Even for Buster
this was something like happiness. Elsewhere
I knew what people were doing to other people,
the terrible hurts, the pleasures of hurting.
I repudiated Zen because it doesn't provide
for forgiveness, repudiated my friend X
who had gotten "in touch with his feelings,"
which were spiteful and aggressive. *Repudiate*
felt good in my mouth, like someone else's tongue
during the sweet combat of love.
I said out loud, *I repudiate*, adding words
like *sincerity, correctness, common sense.*
I remembered how tired I'd grown of mountaintops
and their thin, unheavenly air,
had grown tired, really, of how I spoke of them,
the exaggerated glamor, the false equation between
ascent and importance. I looked at the vase
and its one red flower, then the table
which Zennists would say existed
in its *thisness*, and realized how wrong it was
to reject appearances. How much more difficult
to accept them! I repudiated myself, citing my name.
The phone rang. It was my overly serious friend
from Syracuse saying *Foucault, Foucault,*
like some lost prayer of the tenured.
Advocates of revolution, I agreed with him, poor,
screwed for years, angry—who can begrudge them
weapons and victory? But people like us,
Joan Sutherland on our tapes and enough fine time

to enjoy her, I said, let's be careful
how we link thought and action,
careful about deaths we won't experience.
I repudiated him and Foucault, told him
that if Descartes were alive and wildly in love
he himself would repudiate his famous dictum.
I felt something like happiness when he hung up,
and Buster put his head on my lap,
and without admiration stared at me.
I would not repudiate Buster, not even his fleas.
How could I? Once a day, the flea travels
to the eye of the dog for a sip of water.
Imagine! The journey, the delicacy of the arrival.

BURYING THE CAT

Her name was Isadora and, like all cats,
she was a machine made of rubber bands
and muscle, exemplar of crouch
and pounce, genius of leisure. Seventeen years old.
A neighbor dog had broken her back,
and the owner called when he saw my car
pull into the driveway. He'd put her
in a plastic sack. It was ridiculous
how heavy she was, how inflexible.
For years I've known that to confess
is to say what one doesn't feel. I hereby
confess I was not angry with that dog,
a shepherd, who had seen something foreign
on his property. I'd like to say I was feeling
a sadness so numb that I was a machine myself,
with bad cogs and faulty wiring. But
I'm telling this three years after the fact.
Nothing is quite what it was
after we've formed a clear picture of it.
Behind our house there's a field, a half-acre
of grass good for the sailing of a Frisbee.
I buried her there. My thought was to do it
before the children came home from school,
my wife from work. I got the shovel
from the shed. The ground was not without
resistance. I put several stones on top,
pyramid style, a crude mausoleum. What
we're mostly faced with are these privacies,
inconsequential to all but us. But I wasn't
thinking that then. I kicked some dirt
off the shovel, returned it to the shed.
I remember feeling that strange satisfaction

I'd often felt after yardwork, some evidence
of what I'd done visible for a change.
I remember that after their shock, their grief,
I expected to be praised.

BUSTER'S VISITATION

I'm a dead dog for real now;
no longer can I rise
from my fakery, alert to commands
I'd come to think of as love,
though I never did obey
as well as Sundown did,
or as a truly good dog would.
To play the slave, not be one,
was my code. You understood
who would play the master.
From my grave in the yard I see now
you had no gift for it, or heart.
Bad dog, you'd say,
so little conviction in your voice.
In seconds you'd be patting my head.
Forgiveness made you happy; I'd tip over
the garbage to be forgiven by you.
Let me tell you it's no life
being dead. I'd give anything
to chase the gulls again.
But clarities come when the body goes.
For whatever it's worth
you should know—you who think so much—
only what's been smelled or felt
gets remembered.
And in the dark earth no doors open,
no one ever comes home.

THE ARM

A doll's pink, broken-off arm
was floating in a pond
a man had come to with his dog.
The arm had no sad child nearby
to say it was hers, no parent to rescue it
with a stick or branch,

and this pleased the man to whom
absence always felt like opportunity.
He imagined a girl furious
at her younger sister, taking it out on her
one limb at a time.

Yet the sun was glancing off
the arm's little pink fingers,
and the pond's heart-shaped lily pads
seemed to accentuate an oddness,
which he thought beautiful.

When he and the dog looked for
but couldn't find the doll's body,
a different image came to him,
of a father who hated the fact
that his son liked dolls.
What was floating there

was a punishment that didn't work,
for the boy had come to love
his one-armed doll even more.
Once again the man was struck
by how much misery
the human spirit can absorb.

His dog wanted to move on,
enough of this already.
But the man was creating little waves
with his hands, and the arm, this thing
his wife was sure to question,
was slowly bobbing toward him.

HONESTY

The pines were swaying in the serious wind
   and clouds moved
like white pleasure boats, toward another world.
   There was a drift
of disorder in the air. There was a hint
   of ruckus in the way
the rotting fenceposts kept absolutely still.
   Lucky no one I loved
was nearby; I felt an odd welling up,
   an honesty coming on.
A woodpecker was eating, broadcasting the news.
   You have to have style
to survive such attention to yourself.
   You have to look that good
standing perpendicular as you peck and thunk.
   The serious wind
yielded to the blank otherness of calm.
   I could hear cars
on the Interstate. I could smell my own skin.
   That woodpecker had wings.
After its meal, its noise, it didn't stay around.
   If there isn't a God
maybe there's just a sense we're not
   sufficiently large.
Maybe only through irreverence can we find
   our true size.
That's what I was thinking when my dog came
   carrying a stick.
He wanted to play. He shook his head and tightened
   his grip as if keeping
were fun, possibly generous. Deer were hiding
   in the underbrush.

Only their hungers would make them come out,
  and this wasn't the time,
it wasn't dusk and even the calm wasn't quiet enough.

A PETTY THING

An early frost, and a lone cricket
rubbing his forelegs together, slowly now,
a minor, somewhat courageous sound
in my heartless room where I've come,
heavy-chested, to be alone.
I mean *heatless,* heartless was a slip,
a betrayal really, of the mind.
No doubt the mind wants it to stay.
The cricket reminds me of Eastern Europe,
some bewildered communist holding on.
Now the map-makers, bored for years,
have new squiggly lines to draw.
It's a good time to be Lithuanian—
the cricket has reminded me of this too—
and countless henchmen and torturers
are out of work. Should we feel sad
for their families? I can't decide.
In my heatless room I've been thinking
that the duty-before-pleasure people
balance the books for those of us
dutiful about our pleasures,
and how exemplary crickets are,
playing out their brief summers,
transcending ugliness with song.
The temperature is falling. Night already
has fallen, which is inexact.
Night has come laterally
out of the woods, has risen from the grass.
Everything shy about me loves it,
everything criminal too.

A very petty thing is troubling me,
like one sock missing, though this
is not about socks.
It's so petty I've just been overly polite,
used the famous lie words,
fine and yes and goodnight.
Nearby, I know, mice are squinching
themselves tiny, getting into homes.
They're making important nests
out of dust and hair.
That cricket and the persistent friction
of its rubbing will soon be gone.
It's a sexual song, isn't it,
that crickets sing? They do it to be heard.

Disguised as an Arab, the bouzouki player
introduces her as Fatima, but she's blond,
midwestern, learned to move we suspect
in Continuing Education, Tuesdays, some hip
college town.
We're ready to laugh, this is Aspen
Colorado, cocaine and blue valium
the local hard liquor, and we
with snifters of Mextaca in our hands,
part of the incongruous
that passes for harmony here.
But she's good. When she lets her hair loose,
beautiful. So we revise:
summer vacations, perhaps, in Morocco
or an Egyptian lover, or both.
This much we know:
no Protestant has moved like this
since the flames stopped licking their ankles.
Men rise from dinner tables
to stick dollar bills where their eyes
have been. One slips a five
in her cleavage. When she gets to us
she's dangling money
with a carelessness so vast
it's art, something perfected, all her bones
floating in milk.
The fake Arabs on bongos and bouzouki are real
musicians, urging her, whispering
"Fatima, Fatima," into the mike
and it's true, she has danced the mockery out
of that wrong name in this unlikely place,
she's Fatima and the cheap, conspicuous dreams
are ours, rising now, as bravos.

HERE AND THERE

Here and there nightfall
without fanfare
presses down, utterly
expected, not an omen in sight.
Here and there a husband
at the usual time
goes to bed with his wife
and doesn't dream of other women.
Occasionally a terrible sigh
is heard, the kind that is
theatrical, to be ignored.
Or a car backfires
and reminds us of a car
backfiring, not of a gunshot.
Here and there a man says
what he means and people hear him
and are not confused.
Here and there a missing teenage girl
comes home unscarred.
Sometimes dawn just brings another
day, full of minor
pleasures and small complaints.
And when the newspaper arrives
with the world,
people make kindling of it
and sit together while it burns.

THE STAIRWAY

The architect wanted to build a stairway
and suspend it with silver, almost invisible
guy wires in a high-ceilinged room,
a stairway you couldn't ascend or descend
except in your dreams. But first—
because wild things are not easily seen
if what's around them is wild—
he'd make sure the house that housed it
was practical, built two-by-four by
two-by-four, slat by slat, without ornament.
The stairway would be an invitation
to anyone who felt invited by it,
and depending on your reaction he'd know
if friendship were possible.
The house he'd claim as his, but the stairway
would be designed to be ownerless,
tilted against any suggestion of a theology,
disappointing to those looking for politics.
Of course the architect knew
that over the years he'd have to build
other things the way others desired,
knew that to live in this world was to trade
a few industrious hours for one beautiful one.
Yet every night when he got home
he could imagine, as he walked in the door,
his stairway going nowhere, not for sale,
and maybe some you to whom nothing
about it need be explained, waiting,
the wine decanted, the night about to unfold.

FASCINATIONS

How can we not be fascinated that auks
use their wings to swim underwater,
and flies, those great fliers,
often find themselves stuck
in the bad neighborhood of a web.
Or when a scientist says aphids suck
the life out of plants, and many of us
who don't care about the buzz
of language will not hear
the gorgeous sibilance of esses.
The world is made up of experts
who devote their entire lives
to such little things. They edit magazines
on ant migrations, and examine why
the tiny shit of worms
merits our close attention. And those
deeper thinkers who claim every secret
contains another secret, isn't it true
how often the obvious eludes them?
The man at the casino who plays
double zero at the roulette table
is fascinating, too, as is the pit boss
who believes good luck is a hindrance
to happiness. It's foolish not to believe
that a belief in God is helpful
to those in need of consolation.
Fascinating though, that the prayerful
keep praying, never seem to be disturbed
by the absence of a meaningful connection.

5

LOCAL TIME

The trees were oaks and pines.
The unaffordable house

a little bargain with my soul,
a commitment to the dream

my father lost somewhere
between gin and the dotted line.

The siding was cedar.
The weathervane gun-metal gray.

It was odd how dinner hour
was always approaching,

odd how we counted
what we counted on.

You folded the napkins
in triangles, set the prehistoric

knives and forks. It all seemed
as if it had happened before.

The night came in layers
through the large windows.

When we finished eating
it was wholly there.

The house had double locks
but in the dark a wrong person

would understand: the windows
were made of glass:

the cat wanted out or in,
the cat so easy to impersonate.

We knew that anyone good
would be unafraid of a light

but we turned on the porch light,
left on an inside light

when we went out, advertised
the signs of our presence.

It was what our parents had done
even in a safer time,

it was all their *be carefuls*
awakening inside us

like slow-dissolving pills,
messages in the bloodstream.

Anyone good, we were sure,
would be bold enough

to work in the open,
would give the illusion

he could be tracked down,
identified.

Still, we left the lights on,
parents ourselves now,

deterring with conventional wisdom
the conventional criminal—

no defense against the simple
knock on the door, the man

with a mask so perfect
we'd shake his hand.

Whatever time it was
it was local time, our time.

What was foreign never occurred
until we heard it here,

wasn't that true?
And didn't enough happen here?

The retarded girl nearby
swallowed stones.

Schultz stepped off that ledge,
everyone knew,

because his house wasn't home.
It was exactly seven o'clock

when we got the news—
time for us to hear

and not forget the orbital tick
of the planet, the not-

so-merry-go-round. But for us
there was food every day,

clothing for every season.
The work we did left some time

for the work we loved.
To complain was obscene.

To lament the drift of any day
marked us American, spoiled,

believers in happiness,
the capital I.

The wars in small countries were ours
if the world was ours.

Whether the world was ours
we couldn't decide.

Our neighbor said everything sucked.
It was all humongous, he said,

and I knew what he meant.
Oh on certain days,

when the smoke-screen of weather
or luck permitted,

we loved the world.
Not to love it, risking nothing,

was to fail only at our desks
sulking over commas and typos

or only in the privacies
of bedroom and kitchen

where we lived largely in miniature.
So we loved the world

when we could. No matter,
our house was a hiding place

and the blood dripped in,
deluged and shamed us.

Where would we go?
To work, to the store,

to the next place on the list?—
as if the next place weren't an alarm

set the night before,
as if there always weren't a dream

to give up, something about to happen
to uncomplicated warmth.

I knew after many hurts
how to hold back

what could hurt me,
how to become hollow, absurd.

Passing churches, I remembered
the old repetitions,

the faked novenas,
but what did I feel, really,

after removing disguise after disguise,
then adding others,

could I know what I felt?
At night the shining

steeple across the lake
was a nuisance or a beacon.

Rocky's all-night bar,
just to the south, was oblivion

or a refuge, often both.
Yet the pleasures were near

like ships just offshore, anchored.
I saw them and peopled them,

heard the music and those ahhs
coming through the air, the walls.

I longed to be a visitor
or the visited, and sometimes I was—

wondering, amid touch and entry,
where the music was

and why intimacy carried with it
such distances.

So many times I lifted
the anchor and let it all go—

in my mind
and from this familiar shore.

I turned further inland
toward bric-a-brac, curios,

the narcosis of purchasing.
I turned toward the skillet,

made something for myself.
But I could sense them,

the replacements coming in—
masted, shapely, moving

through old waters calling to me.
You sensed them, too.

One day, finally daring to speak
of soul, wanting to rescue it

from the unnamed
for my own sake, I decided

it wasn't character
but a candle in the room

of character, visible
around the eyes, the mouth.

It was exciting to discover
I was most aware of it

when it was missing, when nothing lived
or burned behind the eyes

and the voice, a tin box,
couldn't support its words.

Only people wrong for us, I decided,
confused soul

with intelligence or with sorrow.
Discussions with them never touched

down, clicked in. In our true friends
there it was, simply.

It became part of what we meant
when we said their names.

It wasn't enough, of course.
Even in the garden I once

believed spectacular, the tulips
were anybody's pretty girl.

The hyacinths offered such small cheer
I turned to the vegetables

as once I turned to foreign films
for the real.

What could I say?
The garden bloomed

but did not transport?
That I wanted my beauty

a little awkward and odd?
Only the moon flower,

among flowers,
pleased me these days,

lily-like,
opening in the dark.

Every hour the clock struck *now*.
It didn't remind us we would die.

The trees needed to be pruned.
You'd prune the trees.

There was no more milk.
I'd get in the car.

Years ago, when the angels
our parents insisted on

could no longer fly
and our bodies took them in,

it seemed we'd solved by cancellation
how to live on our own.

We bought the house,
the house in the cyclic fog

that looked so new.
It's hours now

since a thunderstorm came,
our little world

of tumult and aftermath
seemingly ratified from above.

Though the sky turned perfect
our dog trembled, hid.

Something was out there,
he was sure. The sparrows,

no less foolish or wise,
returned to the yard and sang.

6

ESSAY ON THE PERSONAL

Because finally the personal
is all that matters,
we spend years describing stones,
chairs, abandoned farmhouses—
until we're ready. Always
it's a matter of precision,
what it feels like
to kiss someone or to walk
out the door. How good it was
to practice on stones
which were things we could love
without weeping over. How good
someone else abandoned the farmhouse,
bankrupt and desperate.
Now we can bring a fine edge
to our parents. We can hold hurt
up to the sun for examination.
But just when we think we have it,
the personal goes the way of
belief. What seemed so deep
begins to seem naive, something
that could be trusted
because we hadn't read Plato
or held two contradictory ideas
or women in the same day.
Love, then, becomes an old movie.
Loss seems so common
it belongs to the air,
to breath itself, anyone's.
We're left with style, a particular
way of standing and saying,
the idiosyncratic look

at the frown which means nothing
until we say it does. Years later,
long after we believed it peculiar
to ourselves, we return to love.
We return to everything
strange, inchoate, like living
with someone, like living alone,
settling for the partial, the almost
satisfactory sense of it.

THE VANISHINGS

One day it will vanish,
how you felt when you were overwhelmed
by her, soaping each other in the shower,
or when you heard the news
of his death, there in the T-Bone diner
on Queens Boulevard amid the shouts
of short-order cooks, Armenian, oblivious.
One day one thing and then a dear other
will blur and though they won't be lost
they won't mean as much,
that motorcycle ride on the dirt road
to the deserted beach near Cádiz,
the Guardia mistaking you for a drug-runner,
his machine gun in your belly—
already history now, merely *your* history,
which means everything to you.
You strain to bring back
your mother's full face and full body
before her illness, the arc and tenor
of family dinners, the mysteries
of radio, and Charlie Collins,
eight years old, inviting you
to his house to see the largest turd
that had ever come from him, unflushed.
One day there'll be almost nothing
except what you've written down,
then only what you've written down well,
then little of that.
The march on Washington in '68
where you hoped to change the world
and meet beautiful, sensitive women
is choreography now, cops on horses,

everyone backing off, stepping forward.
The exam you stole and put back unseen
has become one of your stories,
overtold, tainted with charm.
All of it, anyway, will go the way of icebergs
come summer, the small chunks floating
in the Adriatic until they're only water,
pure, and someone taking sad pride
that he can swim in it, numbly.
For you, though, loss, almost painless,
that Senior Prom at the Latin Quarter—
Count Basie and Sarah Vaughan, and you
just interested in your date's cleavage
and staying out all night at Jones Beach,
the small dune fires fueled by driftwood.
You can't remember a riff or a song,
and your date's a woman now, married,
has had sex as you have
some few thousand times, good sex
and forgettable sex, even boring sex,
oh you never could have imagined
back then with the waves crashing
what the body could erase.
It's vanishing as you speak, the soul-grit,
the story-fodder,
everything you retrieve is your past,
everything you let go
goes to memory's out-box, open on all sides,
in cahoots with thin air.
The jobs you didn't get vanish like scabs.
Her good-bye, causing the phone to slip
from your hand, doesn't hurt anymore,
too much doesn't hurt anymore,
not even that hint of your father, ghost-thumping
on your roof in Spain, hurts anymore.

You understand and therefore hate
because you hate the passivity of understanding
that your worst rage and finest
private gesture will flatten and collapse
into history, become invisible
like defeats inside houses. Then something happens
(it is happening) which won't vanish fast enough,
your voice fails, chokes to silence;
hurt (how could you have forgotten?) hurts.
Every other truth in the world, out of respect,
slides over, makes room for its superior.

TALK TO GOD

Thank him for your little house
on the periphery, its splendid view
of the wildflowers in summer,
and the nervous, forked prints of deer
in that same field after a snowstorm.
Thank him even for the monotony
that drives us to make and destroy
and dissect what otherwise would be
merely the lush, unnamed world.
Ease into your misgivings.
Ask him if in his weakness
he was ever responsible
for a pettiness—some weather, say,
brought in to show who's boss
when no one seemed sufficiently moved
by a sunset, or the shape of an egg.
Ask him if when he gave us desire
he had underestimated its power.
And when, if ever, did he realize
love is not inspired by obedience?
Be respectful when you confess to him
you began to redefine heaven
as you discovered certain pleasures.
And sympathize with how sad it is
that awe has been replaced
by small enthusiasms, that you're aware
things just aren't the same these days,
that you wish for him a few evenings
surrounded by the old, stunned silence.
Maybe it will be possible then
to ask, Why this sorry state of affairs?
Why—after so much hatefulness

done in his name—no list of corrections
nailed to some rectory door?
Remember to thank him for the silkworm,
apples in season, photosynthesis,
the northern lights. And be sincere.
But let it be known you're willing to suffer
only in proportion to your errors,
not one unfair moment more.
Insist on this as if it could be granted:
not one moment more.

COMPETITION

Because you played games seriously
   and therefore knew grace
comes hard, rises through the cheap

in us, the petty, the entire history
   of our defeats,
you looked for grace in your opponents,

found a few friends that way
   and so many others
you could never drink with, talk to.

You learned early never to let up,
   never to give
a weaker opponent a gift

because so many times you'd been
   that person
and knew the humiliation in it,

being pandered to, a bone for the sad
   dog.
And because you remembered those times

after a loss when you'd failed
   at grace—
stole from the victor

the pleasures of pure victory
   by speaking
about a small injury or the cold

you weren't quite over—you loved
   those opponents
who'd shake hands and give credit,

save their true and bitter stories
   for their lovers, later,
when all such lamentations are comic,

the sincere *if onlys* of grown men
   in short pants.
Oh there were people who thought

all of it so childish; what to say
   to them, how to agree,
ever, about dignity and fairness?

ARCHAEOLOGY

I tell you nothing new when I say
here we are again, unable to claim
many moments of relief
from the confirmable gloom, though
there was a time, before news became
ubiquitous, when it was possible
to close our eyes and hide in our rooms.
The excitement of bones found
in mass graves—not ours—the remains
of mastodons and dinosaurs, told us
something of our past. Now we see
face down in ditches our neighbors
with whom we once broke bread,
whose children played in our yards,
and everywhere colossal denials of blame.
I tell you nothing new, Andre. I dare
boring you, Miguel, with what
you already know, the enemy
suddenly the enemy, *down on your knees,*
motherfucker, for being down on
your knees to the wrong god.
I dare boring you because the shovels
are blades, the dirt is bloody, and I need
to remind myself of the creatures
we are and have been—remnants
everywhere, no need, really, to dig.

RESPONSE TO A LETTER FROM FRANCE

"We're living in a Socialist paradise.
My mind boggles when I think where you live."

All the trees are in bloom
though the gypsy moths, with their plague
mentality, are blossoming too.
Don't feel sorry for us. We've even learned
to live amid Republicans; the avarice
of gypsy moths is only a little more
mindless, effective. It's okay here.
The ocean isn't perfectly clean
but on good days when I get low enough
the waves push me out ahead of them;
lacking wings or an engine
it's the closest thing to flight.
In France, where life and theory
touch now and then,
I don't doubt your pleasures. But here
there's room enough for incorrect
behavior, which some of us plan on.
There are casinos and fifty or sixty miles
of pines to get lost in.
Socialism makes good sense, sure.
But we actually have four people
who love us, the tennis courts aren't
crowded, our neighbor who has no politics
was generous yesterday for other reasons.
At another time I would offer you
what falls short of promise, the America
outside of me and my part in it.
But not when you feel sorry for us.

I just killed a Brown Recluse spider.
The sun is out. I want you to know
the afternoon is ablaze with ordinary people,
smiling, full of hidden unfulfillment,
everywhere, my friend, everywhere.

South Jersey, July 15, 1981

THE ROUTINE THINGS AROUND THE HOUSE

When Mother died
I thought: now I'll have a death poem.
That was unforgivable

yet I've since forgiven myself
as sons are able to do
who've been loved by their mothers.

I stared into the coffin
knowing how long she'd live,
how many lifetimes there are

in the sweet revisions of memory.
It's hard to know exactly
how we ease ourselves back from sadness,

but I remembered when I was twelve,
1951, before the world
unbuttoned its blouse.

I had asked my mother (I was trembling)
if I could see her breasts
and she took me into her room

without embarrassment or coyness
and I stared at them,
afraid to ask for more.

Now, years later, someone tells me
Cancers who've never had mother love
are doomed and I, a Cancer,

feel blessed again. What luck
to have had a mother
who showed me her breasts

when girls my age were developing
their separate countries,
what luck

she didn't doom me
with too much or too little.
Had I asked to touch,

perhaps to suck them,
what would she have done?
Mother, dead woman

who I think permits me
to love women easily,
this poem

is dedicated to where
we stopped, to the incompleteness
that was sufficient

and to how you buttoned up,
began doing the routine things
around the house.

THAT SATURDAY WITHOUT A CAR

for Ellen Dunn (1910–1969)

Five miles to my mother's house,
a distance I'd never run.
"I *think* she's dead"
my brother said, and hung up

as if with death
language should be mercifully approximate,
should keep the fact
that would forever be fact

at bay. I understood,
and as I ran wondered what words
I might say, and to whom.
I saw myself opening the door—

my brother, both of us, embarrassed
by the sudden intimacy we'd feel.
We had expected it
but we'd expected it every year

for ten: her heart was the best
and worst of her—every kindness
fought its way through damage,
her breasts disappeared

as if the heart itself, for comfort,
had sucked them in.
And I was running better
than I ever had. How different it was

from driving, the way I'd gone
to other deaths—
my body fighting it all off, my heart,
this adequate heart, getting me there.

WHAT GOES ON

After the affair and the moving out,
after the destructive revivifying passion,
we watched her life quiet

into a new one, her lover more and more
on its periphery. She spent many nights
alone, happy for the narcosis

of the television. When she got cancer
she kept it to herself until she couldn't
keep it from anyone. The chemo debilitated
and saved her, and one day

her husband asked her to come back—
his wife, who after all had only fallen
in love as anyone might
who hadn't been in love in a while—

and he held her, so different now,
so thin, her hair just partially
grown back. He held her like a new woman

and what she felt
felt almost as good as love had,
and each of them called it love
because precision didn't matter anymore.

And we who'd been part of it,
often rejoicing with one
and consoling the other,

we who had seen her truly alive
and then merely alive,
what could we do but revise
our phone book, our hearts,

offer a little toast to what goes on.

LEGACY

for my father, Charles Dunn (1905–1967)

1. THE PHOTOGRAPH

My father is in Captain Starns,
a restaurant in Atlantic City.
It's 1950,
I'm there too, eleven years old.
He sold more Frigidaires

than anyone. That's why we're there,
everything free.
It's before the house started
to whisper, before testimony
was called for and lives got ruined.

My father is smiling. I'm smiling.
There's a bowl of shrimp
in front of us.
We have identical shirts on,
short sleeves with little sailboats.
It's before a difference set in

between corniness and happiness.
Soon I'll get up
and my brother will sit next to him.
Mother will click the shutter.
We believe in fairness,

we still believe America
is a prayer, an anthem.

Though his hair is receding
my father's face says nothing
can stop him.

2. THE SECRET

When mother asked him
where the savings went, he said
"the track" and became lost
in his own house, the wastrel,
my mother and her mother
doling out money to him
the rest of his life.

I was sixteen when he told me
the truth, making me his private son,
making anger the emotion
I still have to think about.
I see now that chivalric code
held like a child's song

in the sanctum of his decency,
the error that led to error,
the eventual blur of it all.
And so many nights in the living room
the pages of a newspaper being turned

and his sound—Scotch over ice
in a large glass—how conspicuous
he must have felt,
his best gesture gone wrong,
history changed, the days going on and on.

3. THE FAMILY

The family I was part of
was always extended, grandfather
and grandmother on my mother's side
living with us, and grandfather
with a mistress only my father

knew about, beautiful supposedly
and poor. When she began to die
and wouldn't die fast,
when money became love's test,
grandfather had no one

to turn to except my father
who gave him everything.
It was a pact between men,
a handshake and a secret,
then the country turned

to war and all other debts
must have seemed just personal.
Every night the two of them
huddled by the radio waiting for news
of the clear, identifiable enemy.

4. THE SILENCE

My father became a salesman
heavy with silence.
When he spoke he was charming,
allowed everyone to enjoy
not knowing him.

Nights he'd come home drunk
mother would cook his food
and there'd be silence.
Thus, for years, I thought
all arguments were silent
and this is why silence
is what I arm myself with
and silence is what I hate.

Sleep for him was broken speech,
exclamations, the day come back.
Sleep was the surprise
he'd wake up from, on the couch,
still in his clothes.

I carry silence with me
the way others carry snapshots
of loved ones. I offer it
and wait for a response.

5. THE VISITATION

At the airport, on my way to Spain,
he shook my hand too hard,
said goodbye too long.

I spent his funeral in a room
in Cádiz, too poor to fly back
and paying for what I couldn't afford.

The night he died, the night before
the telegram arrived,
something thumped all night

on the flat roof.
It was my father, I think,
come to be let in.

I was in another country,
living on savings. It must have seemed
like heaven to him.

JUAREZ

For L.

What sad freedom I have,
now that we're unwed.
I can tell the Juarez story,
which you wouldn't let me tell,
though I assured you
I'd tell it as evidence
of the strange places the soul
hides, and why I fell in love.
It was yours, you said. You
wouldn't let me make it mine.
You were in El Paso, a flight
attendant. Between jobs?
I can't quite remember. Men
gravitated to you as if they were
falling apples and you the earth.
This man you were dating, your
El Paso guy, as you called him,
said he knew a whorehouse
in Juarez, a place where
the whores danced and you could
get a table, have drinks, watch.
Let's go, he said, and you did,
with another couple,
parking your car on the U.S. side,
walking in. It was 1961.
You were adventuresome, young.
You didn't know the verb, *to slum*.
You passed an excavation site,
then some adobe shacks, children

barefoot and begging. You passed
a man on a burro. And soon
you were a turista amid the dismal
liveliness of a border town.
Your date was handsome, high-
spirited. You weren't yet sure
if he mattered to you.
The dancing whores had holes
in their underwear. One couldn't
have been more than fifteen.
They danced badly, as if bad
was what everyone wanted—
herky-jerky, lewd. Your date
was clapping. (I remember the face
you made as you said this.)
On the way back, he spoke of the fun
he'd had. Off to your right was
the excavation site.
You didn't know why,
but you climbed down into it as far
as you could go, sat curled up facing
cement blocks, the beginnings
of a foundation. Your friends thought
you a wild woman, a jokester.
But you didn't say anything.
And you wouldn't come up.
For the longest time you wouldn't
come up. Even when they went down
to get you, you wouldn't come up.
I'm sorry. If you hadn't stopped me,
I'd have been telling this
over and over for years.
By now, you'd have corrected
the errors of timing, errors of fact.
It would be that much more yours.

Or maybe you knew that a story
always belongs to its teller,
that nothing you could have said—
once it was told in my voice—
would much matter. Perhaps.
But, after all, it's my story too.
On that dark Juarez night,
every step of your troubled descent
was toward me. I was waiting
in the future for such a woman.

7

HERE AND NOW

for Barbara

There are words
I've had to save myself from,
like My Lord and Blessed Mother,
words I said and never meant,
though I admit a part of me misses
the ornamental stateliness
of High Mass, that smell

of incense. Heaven did exist,
I discovered, but was reciprocal
and momentary, like lust
felt at exactly the same time—
two mortals, say, on a resilient bed,
making a small case for themselves.

You and I became the words
I'd say before I'd lay me down to sleep,
and again when I'd wake—wishful
words, no belief in them yet.
It seemed you'd been put on earth

to distract me
from what was doctrinal and dry.
Electricity may start things,
but if they're to last
I've come to understand
a steady, low-voltage hum

                    of affection
must be arrived at. How else to offset
the occasional slide
into neglect and ill temper?
I learned, in time, to let heaven
go its mythy way, to never again

                be a supplicant
of any single idea. For you and me
it's *here and now* from here on in.
Nothing can save us, nor do we wish
to be saved.

                    Let night come
with its austere grandeur,
ancient superstitions and fears.
It can do us no harm.
We'll put some music on,
open the curtains, let things darken
as they will.

CORNERS

I've sought out corner bars, lived in corner houses;
    like everyone else I've reserved
corner tables, thinking they'd be sufficient.
    I've met at corners
perceived as crossroads, loved to find love
    leaning against a lamp post
but have known the abruptness of corners too,
    the pivot, the silence.
I've sat in corners at parties hoping for someone
    who knew the virtue
of both distance and close quarters, someone with a
    corner person's taste
for intimacy, hard won, rising out of shyness
    and desire.
And I've turned corners there was no going back to,
    corners
in the middle of a room that led
    to Spain or solitude.
And always the thin line between corner
    and cornered,
the good corners of bodies and those severe bodies
    that permit no repose,
the places we retreat to, the places we can't bear
    to be found.

DESIRE

I remember how it used to be
at noon, springtime, the city streets
full of office workers like myself
let loose from the cold
glass buildings on Park and Lex,
the dull swaddling of winter cast off,
almost everyone wanting
everyone else. It was amazing
how most of us contained ourselves,
bringing desire back up
to the office where it existed anyway,
quiet, like a good engine.
I'd linger a bit
with the receptionist,
knock on someone else's open door,
ease myself, by increments,
into the seriousness they paid me for.
Desire was everywhere those years,
so enormous it couldn't be reduced
one person at a time.
I don't remember when it was,
though closer to now than then,
I walked the streets desireless,
my eyes fixed on destination alone.
The beautiful person across from me
on the bus or train
looked like effort, work.
I translated her into pain.
For months I had the clarity
the cynical survive with,
their world so safely small.

Today, walking 57th toward 3rd,
it's all come back,
the interesting, the various,
the conjured life suggested by a glance.
I praise how the body heals itself.
I praise how, finally, it never learns.

SEA LEVEL

Down from the mountains of Appalachia
and the highs of new love
I've come across the extended monotonies
of interstates, back to where
scrub pines stand small at sea level.
There's the house I left for good
(if forever can ever be good),
and there's the Great Egg Harbor river,
which widens here, and everywhere
the visages of ghosts appear
and disappear. I've come to visit
the friends who've stayed
casualty's course—the dearest ones,
who somehow have learned to live
amid the messiness of allegiances,
the turns and half turns of whom now
to console, whom to embrace, and when.
I pull into their driveway, wanting
to tell them how it feels to have—
for the first time—an undivided heart,
a sudden purity of motive,
but when I begin to speak I realize
I don't. I say it anyway, won't take it
back. When their outside cat wants in,
they let him in. Then he wants out.
They accommodate. That cat
is almost as lucky as I. No mountains
here, I can see the afternoon sun
on the horizon hanging on,
about to dip and be gone. Their yard
is a dusty orange. I love the truth,
I swear I do.

AREN'T THEY BEAUTIFUL?

Aren't they beautiful,
she said, with an edge,
because I hadn't commented
on these slender,
some would say splendid
purple things
we'd come upon. The foxgloves,
she repeated, aren't they beautiful?

Foxglove, what a nice name,
I thought, I liked that name,
and told her so, but I was thinking
of conversation, the way *beautiful*
often puts an end to it.
And remembered as a child
those long drives in the country—
Look! a clearing. Look!
a swatch of wildflowers.

All the tedium of ahs and yeses,
all that piety before the perfect.

Beauty, for her, was a beginning,
an honest way in. I knew that,
yet still I wanted to say, Give me
what a troubled soul might see,
give me *that* kind of beautiful,
but heard the sanctimony in it,

told the truth instead, the truth
that also digs one's grave,
becomes its own epitaph.

Until you asked, I said,
I saw nothing, almost nothing.

Deprivation is the mother of beauty,
a wittier man might have declared,
pointing theatrically
to all this blinding abundance.
Or simply admitted he was a prisoner
of his prejudices, helplessly himself.

The foxgloves were looking smug,
uncontestable. And there I was,
impatient, angling for an argument.
We were standing directly in front
of those tall, pendulous eye-catchers.
What do you see now? she asked,
you're staring right at them.

The lies of daylight, the failure of language,
God the vicious, hiding behind another veil.

I place a dead butterfly on the page,
this is called starting
with an image from real life.
It is gold and black
and, as if in some embalmer's dream,
a dusting of talc on its wings.
I have plans
for these wings. I will not let them
slip through my hands.
And if anyone is worried about how
the butterfly died, I'll tell them
my cat swatted it out of the air,
I just picked it up
and brought it to this page
with a notion of breathing
a different life into it. And I confess:
the cat's gesture was more innocent than mine.

The wings suggest nothing I want,
they are so lovely
I simply like the way they distract,
how my eye turns away from the living
room, and the mind spins
into the silliness of spring.
I don't want much.
Just for certain private places
to remain open to me, that's all.
But this is no time to get ethereal.
Already, in a far corner of the page,
something dark is tempting me
to pull it into the poem. One tug

and it's a bat
trapped in sunlight, rabid with fear.

There's no way to keep the ugliness out,
ever. Drops of blood
beautiful, say, on the snow,
always lead to a wound.
Can this still turn out to be a love poem?
Can I still pull you from the wreckage
and kiss your bruises, so black and gold?
Is it too late to introduce you
who were always here, the watermark,
the poem's secret?
From the start all I wanted to explain
was how things go wrong,
how the heart's an empty place
until it is filled,
and how the darkness is forever waiting
for its chance.
If I have failed, know that I was trying
to get to you in my own way,
know that my cat never swatted a butterfly,
it was I who invented and killed it,
something to talk about
instead of you.

IF THE POET

If the poet doesn't yield to the priest,
as Stevens says he shouldn't,
and if both reside in the same small village,
and call on their powers to rectify
or explain the latest disaster,

does the priest become less persuasive
because his ideas are likely not his own,
and is the poet suspect for the same reason?
Would a good priest find the right words,
as the good poet would, in among the many words

passed down for centuries
on what to think, what to believe?
Or would reverence
always get in the way of the true,
thus possibly giving the poet the edge?

That is, if the poet mistrusts words, as he should,
makes them pass hard tests, knows they must
be arranged and shaped in order to convey
even a smidgen of truth, wouldn't he,
although self-ordained, be more reliable?

But what if the villagers believed
they were saved by a prayer the priest said
one Sunday among the ruins? And all the poet
could do was elegize the ruins?
Would the real and the imagined fuse,
become something entirely new?

And what if the poet and priest were one,
each invoking the other as the crops grew
and rain was steady in rainy season, or,
just as confusing, things got worse
and prayers proved useless, and poems
merely decorated the debris where a house

once was? Would it be time for the priest
to admit he'd known but one book? For the poet
to say he'd read many, and look, it hasn't helped?
Or has the issue from the start been a great need
that can't be fully met, only made bearable
and sometimes served by those who try?

AND SO

And so you call your best friend
who's away, just to hear his voice,
but forget his recording concludes
with "Have a nice day."

"Thank you, but I have other plans,"
you're always tempted to respond,
as an old lady once did, the clerk
in the liquor store unable to laugh.

Always tempted, what a sad
combination of words. And so
you take a walk into the neighborhood,
where the rhododendrons are out
and also some yellowy things

and the lilacs remind you of a song
by Nina Simone. "Where's my love?"
is its refrain. Up near Gravel Hill
two fidgety deer cross the road,
whitetails, exactly where

the week before a red fox
made a more confident dash.
Now and then the world rewards,
and so you make your way back

past the careful lawns, the drowsy backyards,
knowing the soul on its own
is helpless, asleep in the hollows
of its rigging, waiting to be stirred.

THE SUDDEN LIGHT AND THE TREES

Syracuse, 1969

My neighbor was a biker, a pusher, a dog
　　and wife beater.
In bad dreams I killed him

and once, in the consequential light of day,
　　I called the Humane Society
about Blue, his dog. They took her away

and I readied myself, a baseball bat
　　inside my door.
That night I heard his wife scream

and I couldn't help it, that pathetic
　　relief; her again, not me.
It would be years before I'd understand

why victims cling and forgive. I plugged in
　　the Sleep-Sound and it crashed
like the ocean all the way to sleep.

One afternoon I found him
　　on the stoop,
a pistol in his hand, waiting,

he said, for me. A sparrow had gotten in
　　to our common basement.
Could he have permission

to shoot it? The bullets, he explained,
  might go through the floor.
I said I'd catch it, wait, give me

a few minutes and, clear-eyed, brilliantly
  afraid, I trapped it
with a pillow. I remember how it felt

when I got it in my hand, and how it burst
  that hand open
when I took it outside, a strength

that must have come out of hopelessness
  and the sudden light
and the trees. And I remember

the way he slapped the gun against
  his open palm,
kept slapping it, and wouldn't speak.

FROM UNDERNEATH

A giant sea turtle saved the life of a 52-year-old woman
lost at sea for two days after a shipwreck
in the Southern Philippines. She rode on the turtle's back.

—SYRACUSE POST-STANDARD

When her arms were no longer
strong enough to tread water
it came up beneath her, hard
and immense, and she thought
this is how death comes,
something large between your legs
and then the plunge.
She dived off instinctively,
but it got beneath her again
and when she realized what it was
she soiled herself, held on.

God would have sent something winged,
she thought. *This* came from beneath,
a piece of hell that killed a turtle
on the way and took its shape.
How many hours passed?
She didn't know, but it was night
and the waves were higher.
The thing swam easily in the dark.

She swooned into sleep.
When she woke it was morning,
the sea calm, her strange raft
still moving. She noticed the elaborate
pattern of its shell, map-like,

the leathery neck and head
as if she'd come up behind
an old longshoreman
in a hard-backed chair.
She wanted and was afraid to touch
the head—one finger
just above the eyes—
the way she could touch her cat
and make it hers.
The more it swam a steady course
the more she spoke to it
the gibberish of the lost.
And then the laughter
located at the bottom
of oneself, unstoppable.

The call went from sailor to sailor
on the fishing boat: A woman
riding an "oil drum"
off the starboard side.
But the turtle was already swimming
toward the prow
with its hysterical, foreign cargo
and when it came up alongside
it stopped
until she could be hoisted off.
Then it circled three times
and went down.
The woman was beyond all language,
the captain reported;
the crew was afraid of her
for a long, long time.

DELINEATION AT DUSK
(FROM "THE SNOWMASS CYCLE")

A lost hour, and that animal lassitude
after a vanished afternoon.
Outside: joggers, cyclists.
Motion, the great purifier, is theirs.
If this were Europe someone in a tower
might be ringing a bell.
People hearing it would know
similar truths, might even know
exactly who they are.
It's getting near drinking time.
It's getting near getting near;
a person alone conjures rules
or can liquefy, fall apart.
That woman with the bouffant—
chewing gum, waiting for the bus—
someone thinks she's beautiful.
It's beautiful someone does.
The sky's murmuring, the storm
that calls you up,
makes promises, never comes.
Somewhere else, no doubt,
a happy man slicing a tomato,
a woman with a measuring cup.
Somewhere else: the foreclosure
of a feeling or a promise,
followed by silence or shouts.
Here, the slow dance of contingency,
an afternoon connected to an evening
by a slender wish. Sometimes absence

makes the heart grow sluggish
and desire only one person, or one thing.
I am closing the curtains.
I am helping the night.

LOVE POEM NEAR THE END OF THE WORLD

This is the world I'm tethered to:
clouds, lavender-tinged, and below them
russet-going-on-green hillsides.
Everywhere various aspirations
of transcendence, like my fickle heart
wishing to redefine itself
as an instrument of hope and generosity,
and flower beds
with just enough rain water
to turn cracked soil into a vast blossoming.
Something keeps me holding on
to a future I didn't think possible.
There's sweetness and there's squalor.
There are sad, almost empty towns
occasionally brightened by fireworks.
And there's you, my love, once volcanic,
beautifully quiet now.

8

HOW TO WRITE A DREAM POEM

Do not try to be faithful.
Change the tunnel to a mountain road
in a South American country, Bolivia
if you need those sounds,
otherwise Chile is a place where
something unfortunate might happen
to someone like you.
Try to avoid elevators descending
at terrible speeds, and though
your predicament should occur
in the evening, do not use dark
except to suggest the complexion
of that young boy
who will report you missing.
A light rain, if you need atmospherics at all.
No thunderstorms, no fallen trees.
So you're on a mountain road
in Chile and you're lost.
Two men wearing fatigues in a jeep
ask you about the weather in heaven,
and you start to run
but you're still standing still, and one of them,
the big one with the mustache and the scar,
hands you what seems like a lily,
freshly cut. Take it, he says, it's yours,
and take this pigeon too, your happiness
is ours. Then they drive away.
It will be important around now
not to mention Bosch or Magritte,
though it will be a good time to wonder
out loud what your dream is about.
Allow yourself to be wrong.

Your readers need to have ideas
of their own, and they will be impatient
with you anyway. Why should we care?
they'll be thinking. What does this
have to do with us?
The large animal that appears out of
the Chilean shadows has someone else
in mind. That blood trail shouldn't be yours.
Jump-cut, perhaps to a tavern
where there's an illusion of safety.
When a toothless woman promises
for a mere kiss that she'll be your guide,
refuse her. She might be
that large animal. Yes, hint that she is.
In dreams shape-shifting is as normal
as fabulous acts of revenge.
But everything in your poem
should depend on arrangement
more than statement, on enchantment
more than any specific, disabling fear.
And when it comes time for you to wake,
no alarm, please. Have the light,
as it does, slowly make you conscious
that it's morning and you're alive.
No problem with being disturbed for a while.
Such things linger. But go down
to breakfast and take your readers with you.
Remember, they're in a world
that's provisional, and yours.
Make some coffee for them. Tell them
the melons are in season, and perfectly chilled.

A SECRET LIFE

Why you need to have one
is not much more mysterious than
why you don't say what you think
at the birth of an ugly baby.
Or, you've just made love
and feel you'd rather have been
in a dark booth where your partner
was nodding, whispering yes, yes,
you're brilliant. The secret life
begins early, is kept alive
by all that's unpopular
in you, all that you know
a Baptist, say, or some other
accountant would object to.
It becomes what you'd most protect
if the government said you can protect
one thing, all else is ours.
When you write late at night
it's like a small fire
in a clearing, it's what
radiates and what can hurt
if you get too close to it.
It's why your silence is a kind of truth.
Even when you speak to your best friend,
the one who'll never betray you,
you always leave out one thing;
a secret life is that important.

DECORUM

She wrote, "They were making love
up against the gymnasium wall,"
and another young woman in class,
serious enough to smile, said

"No, that's fucking, they must
have been fucking," to which many
agreed, pleased to have the proper fit
of word with act.

But an older woman, a wife, a mother,
famous in the class for confusing grace
with decorum and carriage,
said the F-word would distract

the reader, sensationalize the poem.
"Why can't what they were doing
just as easily be called making love?"
It was an intelligent complaint,

and the class proceeded to debate
what's fucking, what's making love,
and the importance of context, tact,
the *bon mot*. I leaned toward those

who favored fucking; they were funnier
and seemed to have more experience
with the happy varieties of their subject.
But then a young man said, now believing

he had permission, "What's the difference,
you fuck 'em and you call it making love;
you tell 'em what they want to hear."
The class jeered, and another man said

"You're the kind of guy who gives fucking
a bad name," and I remembered how fuck
gets dirty as it moves reptilian
out of certain minds, certain mouths.

The young woman whose poem it was,
small-boned and small-voiced,
said she had no objection to fucking,
but these people were making love, it was

her poem and she herself up against
that gymnasium wall, and it felt like love,
and the hell with all of us.
There was silence. The class turned

to me, their teacher, who they hoped
could clarify, perhaps ease things.
I told them I disliked the word fucking
in a poem, but that fucking

might be right in this instance, yet
I was unsure now, I couldn't decide.
A tear formed and moved down
the poet's cheek. I said I was sure

only of "gymnasium," sure it was
the wrong choice, making the act seem
too public, more vulgar than she wished.
How about "boat house?" I said.

BAD

My wife is working in her room,
writing, and I've come in three times
with idle chatter, some not-new news.
The fourth time she identifies me
as what I am, a man lost
in late afternoon, in the terrible
in between—good work long over,
a good drink not yet
what the clock has okayed.
Her mood: a little bemused—
leave-me-the-hell-alone
mixed with a weary smile,
and I see my face
up on the Post Office wall
among Men Least Wanted,
looking forlorn. In the small print
under my name: *Annoying*
to loved ones in the afternoons,
lacks inner resources.
I go away, guilty as charged,
and write this poem, which I insist
she read at drinking time.
She's reading it now. It seems
she's pleased, but when she speaks
it's about charm, and how predictable
I am—how, when in trouble
I try to become irresistible
like one of those blond dogs
with a red bandanna around his neck,
sorry he's peed on the rug.

Forget it, she says, this stuff
is old, it won't work anymore,
and I hear Good boy, Good boy,
and can't stop licking her hand.

TESTIMONY

The Lord woke me in the middle of the night,
and there stood Jesus with a huge tray,
and the tray was heaped with cookies,
and He said, Stephen, have a cookie,

and that's when I knew for sure the Lord
is the real deal, the Man of all men,
because at that very moment
I was thinking of cookies, Vanilla Wafers

to be exact, and there were two
Vanilla Wafers in among the chocolate
chips and the lemon ices, and one
had a big S on it, and I knew it was for me,

and Jesus took it off the tray and put it
in my mouth, as if He were giving me
communication, or whatever they call it.
Then He said, Have another,

and I tell you I thought a long time before I
refused, because I knew it was a test
to see if I were a Christian, which means
a man like Christ, not a big ole hog.

THE 6:10 TO HAPPINESS

is always on time, though the cars
are over-crowded with Americans
in pursuit of what's been promised them.
If you're lucky enough to get on,
it's said that love is only one stop away.
Legends abound. One of them is
the signs for Happiness are obscured
by signs saying Don't Be a Fool
and This Way to Disappointment.

Those who manage to return
say the 6:10 takes months, sometimes years
to arrive, and even the few waiting
with open arms don't speak a language
you've ever heard. But this is the legend
that endures: everyone who comes back
comes alone, some with stories
filled with moments of joy, and even of
relationships that have lasted
beyond the early sexual thrills.

That's why tickets to the 6:10 are always
in demand, and people like myself
who would not mind being fooled
or disappointed if love were the reward,
might pay extra for a window seat,
the better to see in advance the lure
of Happiness, the problematical lay of the land.

JOHN & MARY

John & Mary had never met.
They were like two hummingbirds
who also had never met.

—FROM A FRESHMAN'S SHORT STORY

They were like gazelles who occupied different
grassy plains, running in opposite directions
from different lions. They were like postal clerks
in different zip codes, with different vacation time,
their bosses adamant and clock-driven.
How could they get together?
They were like two people who couldn't get together.
John was a Sufi with a love of the dervish,
Mary of course a Christian with a curfew.
They were like two dolphins in the immensity
of the Atlantic, one playful,
the other stuck in a tuna net—
two absolutely different childhoods!
There was simply no hope for them.
They would never speak in person.
When they ran across that windswept field
toward each other, they were like two freight trains,
one having left Seattle at 6:36 P.M.
at an unknown speed, the other delayed
in Topeka for repairs.
The math indicated that they'd embrace
in another world, if at all, like parallel lines.
Or merely appear kindred and close, like stars.

We were by the hedge that separates our properties
when I asked our neighbors about their souls.
I said it with a smile, the way one asks such a thing.
They were somewhat like us, I thought, more
than middle-aged, less dull than most.
Yet they seemed to have no interest
in disputation, our favorite game,
or any of the great national pastimes
like gossip and stories of misfortunes
about people they disliked.

In spite of these differences, *kindred*
was a word we often felt and used.
The man was shy, though came to life
when he spotted an uncommon bird,
and the woman lively, sometimes even funny
about barometer readings and sudden dips
in pressure, the general state of things.
We liked their affection for each other
and for dogs. We went to their house;
they came to ours.

After I asked about their souls
they laughed and stumbled toward an answer,
then gave up, turned the question back
to me. And because I felt mine always was
in jeopardy, I said it went to the movies
and hasn't been seen since. I said gobbledy
and I said gook. I found myself needing
to fool around, avoid, stay away from myself.

But my wife said her soul suffered from neglect,
that she herself was often neglectful
of important things, but so was I.
Then she started to cry. What's the matter? I asked.
What brought this on? She didn't answer.
I felt ambushed, publicly insensitive
about something, whatever it was.

It was a dusky five o'clock, that time
in between one thing and another.
Our neighbors retreated to their home,
but the woman returned
and without a word put her arms
around my wife as if a woman weeping
indicated something already understood
among women, that needn't be voiced.
They held each other, rocked back and forth,

and I thought *Jesus Christ*, am I guilty again
of one of those small errors
I've repeated until it became large?
What about me? I thought. What about
the sadness of being stupid?
Why doesn't her husband return
with maybe a beer and a knowing nod?

EGGS

I never used to like eggs, that conspicuous
    breaking and ooze like a cow
being slaughtered in the kitchen
    before the steak is served.

And my father wanting his sunny-side-up
    which seemed wrong,
like exposing yourself. But I loved to look
    at unbroken eggs, I loved

to hold them in my hand and toss them up,
    always feeling I knew
how high was too high, always
    coming away clean.

Years later, I'd discover, through Blake,
    you can't get away clean.
You have to know what's more than enough
    to know what's enough,

the game I played was a coward's game.
    I liked my eggs hard boiled
at first, then deviled, ice cold.
    Scrambled was years off;

breaking and cooking them myself—more years.
    One Halloween I stole eggs
from the egg farm, extra large, to throw at girls.
    Loving the shape of eggs,

confused by the shape of girls, I loved
   to see the egg break
on their jeans, loved the screams and the stain.
   Now I suck eggs

after making a little hole in the tip.
   I've made peace with the yolk.
I no longer think of the whites as coming
   face to face with the blind.

I almost can forget how the conglomerates
   have made chickens slaves,
the small cages and the perpetual light.
   I love eggs now,

I love women; I keep my eggs to myself.
   As for the chicken and the egg
I say the egg was first. The egg is perfect.
   It always was.

The chicken, like most children, an afterthought.

SHATTERINGS

In my dream I'm addressing a large class
about Trotsky and Rimbaud. Trotsky
wanted perpetual revolution, I tell them,
Rimbaud a derangement of the senses.
Wouldn't it be fun to have dinner with them?

Most of my students have forsaken home,
or are planning to. They don't want
to have dinner with anybody.
They've mastered the boredom
they think conceals them. But the hungers

of the few are palpable, they're famished
for the marrow of experience, for the yet
to arrive viscera of their historical moment.
Rimbaud is now twenty-two, I say,
gunrunning in Africa. He's already given up

poetry, grown tired of breaking its rules.
Trotsky has fled to Mexico. Stalin's thugs
will soon cross the border with their ice axes.
My class is called Whatever I Feel Like
Talking About. No matter what the subject,

over the years it's been the only course
I've ever taught. Meanwhile, a rose explodes
on the chalkboard, three crows caw a hole
in the sky. My job is to shatter a few things.
Should I put them back together?

What's going on here? What kind of dream
with Rimbaud in it finds itself concerned
with responsibility? Yet I ask,
What's the responsibility of the lyric poet?
How it feels being himself? Why should

anyone care? And the political philosopher,
shouldn't he know a wildness can't go on forever?
Perpetual anything, I say, give me a break.
Just how many deaths can a good idea justify?
This dream is in need of a boutonniere,

or maybe a bullet suspended in midair.
But just in time a student rises and says,
In the spirit of Trotsky, let's tear up
all our notes from this class-ridden class,
let's caress the world with leaflets.

Half of the class follows him out the door.
Clearly, I've poorly educated the others
who remain seated, terrified they can't find
what's next on the syllabus.
But there, isolated among them, is that boy,

my Rimbaudian, all testosterone and refusal,
the one I always teach to, look how
he shrugs and heads toward the exit
as if the future already had assured him
it has openings for someone so unafraid of it,

his assignments unfinished, his grade in doubt.

MON SEMBLABLE

No man has ever dared
to describe himself as he truly is.

—ALBERT CAMUS

I like things my way
every chance I get.
A limit doesn't exist

when it comes to that.
But please, don't confuse
what I say with honesty.

Isn't honesty the open yawn
the unimaginative love
more than truth?

Anonymous among strangers
I look for those
with hidden wings,

and for scars
that those who once had wings
can't hide.

Though I know it's unfair,
I reveal myself
one mask at a time.

Does this appeal to you,
such slow disclosures,
a lifetime perhaps

of almost knowing one another?
I would hope you, too,
would hold something back,

and that you'd always want
whatever unequal share
you had style enough to get.

Altruism is for those
who can't endure their desires.
There's a world

as ambiguous as a moan,
a pleasure moan
our earnest neighbors

might think a crime.
It's where we could live.
I'll say I love you,

which will lead, of course,
to disappointment,
but those words unsaid

poison every next moment.
I will try to disappoint you
better than anyone ever has.

BECOMING ONESELF

Occasionally, after vowing to shut down
a few of my lesser selves, I'd try to behave
like a honey bee in a hive, working for the good
of the queen, therefore the entire enterprise.

But I couldn't help but think of the politics
I was entertaining and the implications
of a singular, mindless, deadly obeisance
to one great leader. And I was sure if

I gave up certain petty parts of myself
I'd miss the pleasures of spreading rumors,
and my inquisitions of the pious,
not to mention the witnessing of utopias

sliding inevitably into monarchies.
Of course the queen was just being herself,
a pollinator, who wouldn't hurt another creature
unless provoked, as opposed to her predatory

cousin, the wasp, also being itself,
with the power to sting more than once.
Isn't it all just Nature anyway,
no one either bad or good?

No such luck for people like me,
always wishing to be one thing
while thinking another, kindly one day,
waspy another, judgmental, human.

At breakfast this morning I told a woman
named Dalit that right outside my window
a bird had been singing her name.
No doubt it meant I'd been thinking of her,
and she seemed pleased. I suppose the bird
could have been singing Larry,
had I been thinking of him. But, no,
I was sure it kept repeating *Da-lit, Da-lit.*
Years ago I resolved to try hard
not to become like the whip-poor-will,
its beautiful lilt turning monotonous
as it kept calling out its own name.
I'd try to be like a mockingbird instead,
the one that included in its repertoire
many birds as well as the meow of my cat.
At dinner last night some of us were listing
books that we hate. I couldn't think of any,
so I made one up. Dalit wasn't present.
Da-lit, Da-lit. A mockingbird never stops
including, though often it may seem
unoriginal, indiscriminate, inordinately
pleased with itself. But why shouldn't it?
Imagine how surprise turns into delight
as each time it sings it hears another voice.
After many mornings, it is all of its voices.
What fascinates? How do we know
what we love? I trespass, steal, accumulate,
I do what the mockingbird does.

9

LOOSESTRIFE

1

Storms moved across the Rockies
and through the plains, rode the jet stream
east. By the time they reached us: rain.
And there were other things that looked—
to other eyes—like welcome news.
The country tilting right.
A few more punishments for the poor.
It was the winter winter never came
to South Jersey; no natural equivalent,
once again, to our lives. All around us
a harshness, a severity, not destined soon
to stop. Oh we were part of it,
reserved ourselves for just a few,
held back instead of gave. Our hearts:
caged things, no longer beating
for the many, who were too many now.
Meanwhile, the Dakotas were snowed in.
A bad wind came off the lakes,
and Chicago and Buffalo braced
for a familiar misery, predictable,
the satisfaction, at least, of what was due.
Here the sun came out and stayed for days.
It wasn't cold enough to think of warmth.
For months, it seemed, we lived lower
in the nation, seasonless, the answers
mostly Christian, though far from Christlike,
to every hard and bitter question.

2

The impatient, upstart crocuses
and daffodils fell once again
for the lies of March.
They simply wanted to exist.
The warm sun must have said Now,
and they gave themselves
to that first, hardly refusable touch.
History was whispering
at least another frost,
but who listens to the hushed sobrieties
of the old? The daffodils died
the advantaged death
of those with other deaths to live.
We stripped down, got colds.
Heraclitus, I want to say I've stepped
into the same stream twice,
and everything felt the same.
It wasn't, I know that now,
but what it felt like
had a truth of its own.
The daffodils and crocuses
traveled through the solitude
of what they felt
toward what they might become.
Choiceless, reactive, inhuman—
nothing to admire in what they did.

3

A superior sky mottled in the west,
the water beneath it glassy, still.
As I crossed the bridge, there it was:
the landscape's invitation to forget.

An osprey swooped low, disreputable
as birds go, but precise, efficient,
a banker in wing-tips, office-bound,
ready to foreclose.
We live in a postcard, I thought,
cropped, agreeably, to deceive;
beyond its edges
broken glass at the schoolyard,
routine boredom, decency, spite.
And then the white, wood-framed
colonials on either side of 575,
Sinton's apple orchard, the shack
with three old cars in front of it,
its porch slanted, no one ever home.
The mowed field and the field wild
with rockrose and goat's rue
declared themselves as property, ours,
no one else's, and I acknowledged
how good the differentiating spaces were
between people and people,
I, who, years ago—
acolyte to an era's pious clarities—
went home to accuse
my dear parents of being capitalists.

4

Clear nights I looked upward and said,
"My God," a figure of speech,
another exhalation of surprise.
The sky was enormous, a planetarium
without walls, the stars free of charge.
Its mythy inhabitants were loose in us,
free-floating energies, nameless now.
It was April, unusually dry.

Forest fires moved through the Barrens.
We needed rain and got wind.
Once we'd have prayed, and gotten wind.
The fires reached Batsto, were stopped
in time, though our time would come.
How to live as if it would? Deeper? Wilder?
Yard sale on Clark's Landing Road.
Raffle at the church. My own yard needing
the care a good citizen would give it.
Thousands of quiet ways gradually to die.
I drove eight miles to the fire's edge.
Planes dropping water had stopped it
and a turn in the wind
and men with shovels and courage.
They didn't need to dig deep, but wide.
It was beyond them, what they had done.

5

Pascal, even your century compelled you
to feel, "We wander in times not ours."
There were authorities in those days,
there were soul-maps; it's heartening
you knew they couldn't be yours.
Here a four-wheel drive can make it through
our wilderness. The hunter-worn paths
instruct us where to turn. It seems
that much harder to get good and lost.
I dream of the rumored secret road
in Warren Grove, at the end of which
a canoe waits, and miles of winding river.
Dream, too, of the rumored Satanists there
and cats and dogs disemboweled.
I think, Pascal, you would feel
little has changed.

Cherry and apple blossoms can't distract us
long enough, or streets charged
with beautiful body, beautiful face.
Still, I can't be sure, as you were,
that what's hidden is any more mysterious
than the palpable immensity that isn't.

6

The winter winter never came—like memory
itself—moved from fact to language,
a coloration of what was seen and felt.
My ear still liked winter's doubling.
My eye was fond of its nearness to mistake.
Yet the made world had turned
to the stirrings of grass and insect,
to Oklahoma City bereft.
How little moral effort it takes to open,
then close our hearts! I found myself inclined
now to incident, now to words, conflicted,
like someone besot with spices and sauce,
wishing to stay thin.
The weather urged us out, away from worry,
that indoor work. Cut-offs and rollerblades
met us daringly at the curb, American
as pick-up trucks with rifle racks.
If we walked far enough and looked:
loosestrife, goldenrod, pixie-moss.
I knew loosestrife, I knew so many such things
before I knew their names.

7

Mornings I used to walk the dogs
by Nacote Creek, months before their deaths,
I'd see the night's debris, the tide's vagaries,
the furtive markings of creatures desperate
to eradicate every smell not theirs.
I understood those dogs, who had so little
of their own. Why not perfume
a rock, make a bush redolent
of their best selves? The boat launch
slanted waterward. The dogs avoided it,
bred for land, doomed to sniff
and cover-up and die—brothers, mine.
This was the town beach, where soon
children would vie with sandpiper and gull.
Every month, like every mind,
changed the way things looked.
I miss those mornings of the dogs.
Winter will be less wind-swept and personal
from now on, spring less observed.

8

Owned by the mayor's brother,
out of earshot of the Zoning Board's
center-of-town houses: The Shooting Place.
Farm-raised quail let loose like mice
for lazy cats, then the shotguns' heavy-metal.
Elsewhere, of course, the quail were kids
who'd gotten in the way of gangs
or their parents' close-quartered rage.
We protested anyway.
In Atlantic City, ten miles southeast,
the marshland gave way to slums

and bright lights. All nature there was human.
The six o'clock news showed the results.
Back here: pitchpine, crowberry, black oak.
Even the directions to The Shooting Place
made us want to say them. Down Chestnut Neck
to Red Wing Lake. Right at the campground.
Gone too far if you reach Beaver Run.

9

A philosopher, musing cosmically, might think
we were people who needed to be disturbed,
would say no truth ever reveals itself
to those sipping something on their porch.
I hated the cosmic as I hated a big sound
on a quiet afternoon. And I was disturbed enough,
or thought I was, for a hundred truths
to come show their wounded, open hearts.
Where were they then?
Our margaritas were rimmed with salt.
It was 5 p.m. Time even for philosophers—
sure of shelter and sufficient bread—
to take off their shoes, settle in.
Far away, men were pulling bodies from debris,
a moan the sweetest, most hopeful thing.

10

It's been their time—this winter's spring—
the shooters and the complainers
on a side not mine. They wanted America
theirs again, they said, and shouted their votes.
Mice abandoned their ingenious, fluffy homes
in attics and storage rooms, returned
to the fields. Every owl in the county knew.

Everything that couldn't think and everything
that could had made sensible plans.
At school, because it was his bold time,
a home-grown senior hot for elsewhere
asked why I stayed in South Jersey.
"Because it hasn't been invented yet," I said.
Where he saw nothing, I saw chance.
But I should have said in flat country
friends are mountains, that a place sometimes
is beautiful because of who was good to you
in the acrimonious air. So hard not to lie.
I should have said this landscape,
lush and empty and so undreamed,
is the party to which we bring our own.
I should have kept talking until I'd gotten it true.
Something about what the mouse doesn't know
and the owl does. Something intolerable
like that, with which we live.

10

BEFORE THE STORM

A slight breeze, then something
like a murmur among the leaves
and up above clouds on the verge
of a good cry, lightning all around.
These are the forerunners
of what could be a familiar occurrence,
but I like to throw out
then try to hold back
the rest of the story, always unsure
of what comes next.
Let the wind accelerate; I'll pay it
no mind. Let the moon
take the ocean for a ride.
I want to be the man
who as he speaks finds
what he thinks, whose confessions
implicate everyone, no excuses,
no one's parade spared.

STORY

A woman's taking her late-afternoon walk
on Chestnut where no sidewalk exists
and houses with gravel driveways
sit back among the pines. Only the house
with the vicious dog is close to the road.
An electric fence keeps him in check.
When she comes to that house, the woman
always crosses to the other side.

I'm the woman's husband. It's a problem
loving your protagonist too much.
Soon the dog is going to break through
that fence, teeth bared, and go for my wife.
She will be helpless. I'm out of town,
helpless too. Here comes the dog.
What kind of dog? A mad dog, a dog
like one of those teenagers who just loses it
on the playground, kills a teacher.

Something's going to happen that can't happen
in a good story: out of nowhere a car
comes and kills the dog. The dog flies
in the air, lands in a patch of delphiniums.
My wife is crying now. The woman who hit
the dog has gotten out of her car. She holds
both hands to her face. The woman who owns
the dog has run out of her house. Three women
crying in the street, each for different reasons.

All of this is so unlikely; it's as if
I've found myself in a country of pure fact,
miles from truth's more demanding realm.
When I listened to my wife's story on the phone
I knew I'd take it from her, tell it
every which way until it had an order
and a deceptive period at the end. That's what
I always do in the face of helplessness,
make some arrangements if I can.

Praise the odd, serendipitous world.
Nothing I'd be inclined to think of
would have stopped that dog.
Only the facts saved her.

THE WAITING

I waited for you calmly, with infinite patience.
I waited for you hungrily, just short of desperate.

When you came I knew that desperate was unattractive.
I was calm, no one wants the kind of calm I was.

It tried your patience, it made you hungry for a man
who was hungry. I am that man, I said,

but I said it calmly. My body was an ache, a silence.
It could not affirm how long it had waited for you.

It could not claw or insist or extend its hands.
It was just a stupid body, closed up and voracious.

IN LOVE, HIS GRAMMAR GREW

In love, his grammar grew
rich with intensifiers, and adverbs fell
madly from the sky like pheasants
for the peasantry, and he, as sated
as they were, lolled under shade trees
until roused by moonlight
and the beautiful fraternal twins
and and *but*. Oh that was when
he knew he couldn't resist
a conjunction of any kind.
One said *accumulate*, the other
was a doubter who loved the wind
and the mind that cleans up after it.
           For love
he wanted to break all the rules,
light a candle behind a sentence
named Sheila, always running on
and wishing to be stopped
by the hard button of a period.
Sometimes, in desperation, he'd look
toward a mannequin or a window dresser
with a penchant for parsing.
But mostly he wanted you, Sheila,
and the adjectives that could precede
and change you: *bluesy, fly-by-night,*
queen of all that is and might be.

TENDERNESS

Back then when so much was clear
and I hadn't learned
young men learn from women

what it feels like to feel just right,
    I was twenty-three,
she thirty-four, two children, a husband

in prison for breaking someone's head.
Yelled at, slapped
around, all she knew of tenderness

was how much she wanted it, and all
    I knew
were back seats and a night or two

in a sleeping bag in the furtive dark.
We worked
in the same office, banter and loneliness

leading to the shared secret
    that to help
National Biscuit sell biscuits

was wildly comic, which led to my body
    existing with hers
like rain that's found its way underground

to water it naturally joins.
    I can't remember
ever saying the exact word, tenderness,

though she did. It's a word I see now
    you must be older to use,
you must have experienced the absence of it

often enough to know what silk and deep balm
    it is
when at last it comes. I think it was terror

at first that drove me to touch her
    so softly,
then selfishness, the clear benefit

of doing something that would come back
    to me twofold,
and finally, sometime later, it became

reflexive and motiveless in the high
    ignorance of love.
Oh abstractions are just abstract

until they have an ache in them. I met
    a woman never touched
gently, and when it ended between us

I had new hands and new sorrow,
    everything it meant
to be a man changed, unheroic, floating.

SWEETNESS

Just when it has seemed I couldn't bear
    one more friend
waking with a tumor, one more maniac

with a perfect reason, often a sweetness
    has come
and changed nothing in the world

except the way I stumbled through it,
    for a while lost
in the ignorance of loving

someone or something, the world shrunk
    to mouth-size,
hand-size, and never seeming small.

I acknowledge there is no sweetness
    that doesn't leave a stain,
no sweetness that's ever sufficiently sweet . . .

Tonight a friend called to say his lover
    was killed in a car
he was driving. His voice was low

and guttural, he repeated what he needed
    to repeat, and I repeated
the one or two words we have for such grief

until we were speaking only in tones.
    Often a sweetness comes
as if on loan, stays just long enough

to make sense of what it means to be alive,
    then returns to its dark
source. As for me, I don't care

where it's been, or what bitter road
    it's traveled
to come so far, to taste so good.

STONE SEEKING WARMTH

Look, it's usually not a good idea
to think seriously about me.
I've been known to give others
a hard time. I've had wives and lovers—
trust that I know a little about trying
to remain whole while living
a divided life. I don't easily open up.
If you come to me, come to me
so warned. I am smooth and grayish.
It's possible my soul is made of schist.

But if you are not dissuaded by now,
well, my door is ajar. I don't care
if you're in collusion with the wind.
Come in, there's nothing here
but solitude and me. I wouldn't mind
being diminished one caress at a time.

LANGUAGE: A LOVE POEM

After Neruda

When I say your hair
is the color of a moonless night
in which I've often been lost,
I mean approximately that dark.
And the dove outside our window
is no symbol, merely wakes us
at dawn, its mate a grayish creature
that coos quite poorly. Peace
is an entirely different bird.
The rose, to me, signifies the rose,
and the guitar signifies
a musical instrument
called the guitar. At other times
language is a slaughterhouse,
a hammering down, its subjects hanging
from hooks, on the verge
of being delicious. When I say
these things to you it's to watch
how certain words play
themselves out on your face,
as if no one with imagination
can ever escape being a witness.
The whale, for example, no matter
its whiteness, is just a mammal
posing as a big fish, except
of course if someone is driven
to pursue it. That changes everything.

Which is not to suggest I don't love
the depth of your concealments.
When I say your name over and over
it's because I cannot possess you.

PRIVILEGE

. . . the privilege of ordinary heartbreak
—NADEZHDA MANDELSTAM

I have had such privilege
    and have wept
the admittedly small tears

that issue from it, and for years
    have expected
some terrible random tax

for being born or staying alive.
    It has not come,
though recently in the neighborhood

a child's red ball got loose
    from her, with traffic
bearing down. She was not my child,

I was so happy she was not
    my child.
If one could choose, who wouldn't

settle for deceit or betrayal,
    something
that could be argued or forgiven?

And when I think of Osip, his five
    thousand miles
on a prison train, and the package

you sent him returned months later,
   "The addressee is dead,"
well, that's when the mind that hunts

for comparisons should hesitate,
   then seek
its proper silence. History pressed in

and down, Nadezhda, and you kept living
   and found the words.
I intend no comparison when I say

today the odor of lilacs outside
   my window
is half perfume, half something rotten.

That's just how they smell
   and what I'm used to,
one thing and always the disturbing

insistence of another, fat life itself,
   too much
to let in, too much to turn away.

ACHILLES IN LOVE

There was no getting to his weakness.
In public, even in summer, he wore
big boots, specially made for him,
a band of steel reinforcing each heel.
At home, when he bathed or slept,
he kept a pistol within reach, loaded.
And because to be invulnerable
is to be alone, he was alone even when
he was with you. You could sense it
in the rigidity of his carriage, as if under
his fine-fitting suits were layers of armor.
Yet everyone loved to see him in action:
While his enemies were thinking of small
advantages, he only thought end game.

Then she came along, who seemed to be all
women fused into one, cheekbones and breasts
evidence that evolution doesn't care
about fairness, and a mind so good, well,
it was like his. You could see his body soften,
and days later, when finally they were naked,
she instinctively knew what to do—
as smart men do with a mastectomy's scar—
to kiss his heel before kissing
what he considered to be his power,
and with a tenderness that made him tremble.

And so Achilles began to live differently.
Both friends and enemies were astounded
by his willingness to listen, and hesitate
before responding. Even in victory he'd
walk away without angering a single god.

He wore sandals now because she liked him in sandals.
He never felt so exposed, or so open to the world.
You could see in his face something resembling terror,
but in fact it was love, for which he would die.

THE IMAGINED

If the imagined woman makes the real woman
seem bare-boned, hardly existent, lacking in
gracefulness and intellect and pulchritude,
and if you come to realize the imagined woman
can only satisfy your imagination, whereas
the real woman with all her limitations
can often make you feel good, how, in spite
of knowing this, does the imagined woman
keep getting into your bedroom, and joining you
at dinner, why is it that you always bring her along
on vacations when the real woman is shopping,
or figuring the best way to the museum?

                        And if the real woman

has an imagined man, as she must, someone
probably with her at this very moment, in fact
doing and saying everything she's ever wanted,
would you want to know that he slips in
to her life every day from a secret doorway
she's made for him, that he's present even when
you're eating your omelette at breakfast,
or do you prefer how she goes about the house
as she does, as if there were just the two of you?
Isn't her silence, finally, loving? And yours
not entirely self-serving? Hasn't the time come,

                     once again, not to talk about it?

BEAUTIFUL WOMEN

More things come to them,
and they have more to hide.
All around them: mirrors, eyes.
　　　　In any case
they are different from other women
and like great athletes have trouble
making friends, and trusting a world
quick to praise.

I admit without shame
I'm talking about superficial beauty,
the beauty unmistakable
to the honest eye, which causes
some of us to pivot and to dream,
to tremble before we dial.

　　Intelligence warmed by generosity
is inner beauty, and what's worse
some physically beautiful women have it,
and we have to be strapped and handcuffed
to the mast, or be ruined.

But I don't want to talk of inner beauty,
it's the correct way to talk
and I'd feel too good
about myself, like a parishioner.
　　　　Now, in fact,
I feel like I'm talking
to a strange beautiful woman at a bar, I'm
animated, I'm wearing that little fixed
smile, I might say anything at all.

Still, it's better to treat a beautiful woman
as if she were normal, one of many.
She'll be impressed that you're unimpressed,
might start to lean your way.
This is especially true if she has aged
into beauty, for she will have learned
the sweet gestures one learns
in a lifetime of seeking love.
Lucky is the lover of such a woman
and lucky the woman herself.

Beautiful women who've been beautiful girls
are often in some tower of themselves
waiting for us to make the long climb.

But let us have sympathy for the loneliness
of beautiful women.
Let us have no contempt for their
immense privilege, or for the fact
that they never can be wholly ours.

It is not astonishing
when the scared little girl in all of them
says here I am, or when they weep.
But we are always astonished by what
beautiful women do.

"Boxers punch harder when women are around,"
Kenneth Patchen said. Think what happens
when *beautiful* women are around.
We do not question
that a thousand ships were launched.

In the eye of the beholder? A platitude.
A beautiful woman enters a room,
and everyone beholds. Geography changes.
We watch her everywhere she goes.

THE HOUSE WAS QUIET

After Stevens

The house was quiet and the world vicious,
peopled as it is with those deprived
of this or that necessity, and with weasels, too,
and brutes, who don't seem to need
a good excuse. The house was quiet as if it knew
it was being split. There was a sullenness
in its quiet. A hurt. The house was us.
It wasn't a vicious house, not yet. We hadn't
yet denuded its walls, rolled up its rugs.
It had no knowledge of the world
and thus of those who, in the name of justice,
would ransack belongings, cut throats.
Once the house had resounded with stories.
Now it was quiet, it was terrible how quiet it was.
And, sensing an advantage, the world pressed in.

FIVE ROSES IN THE MORNING

March 16, 2003

On TV the showbiz of war,
so I turn it off
wishing I could turn it off,
and glance at the five white roses
in front of the mirror on the mantel,
looking like ten.
That they were purchased out of love
and are not bloody red
won't change a goddamned thing—
goddamned things, it seems, multiplying
every day. Last night
the roses numbered six, but she chose
to wear one in her hair,
and she was more beautiful
because she believed she was.
It changed the night a little.
For us, I mean.

11

EACH FROM DIFFERENT HEIGHTS

That time I thought I was in love
and calmly said so
was not much different from the time
I was truly in love
and slept poorly and spoke out loud
to the wall
and discovered the hidden genius
of my hands.
And the times I felt less in love,
less than someone,
were, to be honest, not so different
either.
Each was ridiculous in its own way
and each was tender, yes,
sometimes even the false is tender.
I am astounded
by the various kisses we're capable of.
Each from different heights
diminished, which is simply the law.
And the big bruise
from the longer fall looked perfectly white
in a few years.
That astounded me most of all.

THANK YOU,

dear, for taking our granddaughter Samantha
to the carnival, and then to the park
with monkey bars and swings.
I haven't been lemur-like for years,
and I no longer wish to push kids toward heaven,
even if they swing back to earth
fascinated and unchurchly—as I wish
them to be. Samantha believes in monsters
both good and bad, sweet things
with strange hungers. Keep this in mind
when at the carnival you introduce her
to the fun house meant to distort and please.
Try to smile at how grotesque you become,
and, for my sake, tell her her grandfather
is always looking for mirrors that give back
something other than himself. I'd tell her
myself, but I'm happily here, hiding out
in our house where today the fun for me
is not going to any carnival or park.
So smart of you to leave me behind.
I would have lagged with lack of interest,
perhaps declared one or two alienable rights.
Thank you for knowing my tendencies,
which are not to be admired, I realize,
though I love that you honor them
some of the time. When Samantha grows up,
doing for herself what she has learned
from me, let's hope someone like you
understands monkey business trumps duty
most days of the week. Is that true?—
a voice cannot help but ask.

Thank you anyway for taking her
to these places where other children gather,
and enjoy themselves so fully it seems
they never wonder why their grandfathers
are elsewhere. But that same voice says,
doesn't every heart have a ledger,
isn't every absence an event to be recorded?

DANCING WITH GOD

At first the surprise
of being singled out,
the dance floor crowded
and me not looking my best,
a too-often-worn dress
and the man with me
a budding casualty
of one repetition too much.
God just touched his shoulder
and he left.
Then the confirmation of
an old guess:
God was a wild god,
into the most mindless rock,
but graceful,
looking—this excited me—
like no one I could love,
cruel mouth, eyes evocative
of promises unkept.
I never danced better, freer,
as if dancing were my way
of saying how easily
I could be with him, or apart.
When the music turned slow
God held me close
and I felt for a moment
I'd mistaken him,
that he was Death
and this the famous embrace
before the lights go out.
But God kept holding me
and I him

until the band stopped
and I stood looking at a figure
I wanted to slap
or forgive for something,
I couldn't decide which.
He left then, no thanks,
no sign
that he'd felt anything
more than an earthly moment
with someone who could've been
anyone on earth.
To this day I don't know why
I thought he was God,
though it was clear
there was no going back
to the man who brought me,
nice man
with whom I'd slept
and grown tired,
who danced wrong,
who never again
could do anything right.

THE GUARDIAN ANGEL

Afloat between lives and stale truths,
    he realizes
he's never truly protected one soul,

they all die anyway, and what good
    is solace,
solace is cheap. The signs are clear:

the drooping wings, the shameless thinking
    about utility
and self. It's time to stop.

The guardian angel lives for a month
    with other angels,
sings the angelic songs, is reminded

that he doesn't have a human choice.
    The angel of love
lies down with him, and loving

restores to him his pure heart.
    Yet how hard it is
to descend into sadness once more.

When the poor are evicted, he stands
    between them
and the bank, but the bank sees nothing

in its way. When the meek are overpowered
    he's there, the thin air
through which they fall. Without effect

he keeps getting in the way of insults.
He keeps wrapping
his wings around those in the cold.

Even his lamentations are unheard,
    though now,
in for the long haul, trying to live

beyond despair, he believes, he needs
    to believe
everything he does takes root, hums

beneath the surfaces of the world.

BETWEEN ANGELS

Between angels, on this earth
absurdly between angels, I
try to navigate

in the bluesy middle ground
of desire and withdrawal,
in the industrial air,
among the bittersweet

efforts of people to connect,
make sense, endure.
The angels out there,
what are they?

Old helpers, half-believed,
or dazzling better selves,
imagined,

that I turn away from
as if I preferred
all the ordinary, dispiriting
tasks at hand?

I shop in the cold
neon aisles
thinking of pleasure,
I kiss my paycheck

a mournful kiss goodbye
thinking of pleasure,
in the evening replenish

my drink, make a choice
to read or love or watch,
and increasingly I watch.
I do not mind living

like this. I cannot bear
living like this.
Oh, everything's true
at different times

in the capacious day,
just as I don't forget
and always forget

half the people in the world
are dispossessed.
Here chestnut oaks
and tenements

make their unequal claims.
Someone thinks of betrayal.
A child spills her milk;
I'm on my knees cleaning it up—

sponge, squeeze, I change nothing,
just move it around.
The inconsequential floor
is beginning to shine.

LONG TERM

On this they were in agreement:
everything that can happen between two people
happens after a while

or has been thought about so hard
there's almost no difference
between desire and deed.

Each day they stayed together, therefore,
was a day of forgiveness, tacit,
no reason to say the words.

It was easy to forgive, so much harder
to be forgiven. The forgiven had to agree
to eat dust in the house of the noble

and both knew this couldn't go on for long.
The forgiven would need to rise;
the forgiver need to remember the cruelty

in being correct.
Which is why, except in crises,
they spoke about the garden,

what happened at work,
the little ailments and aches
their familiar bodies separately felt.

HAPPINESS

A state you must dare not enter
    with hopes of staying,
quicksand in the marshes, and all

the roads leading to a castle
    that doesn't exist.
But there it is, as promised,

with its perfect bridge above
    the crocodiles,
and its doors forever open.

ALL THAT WE HAVE

for John Jay Osborn, Jr.

It's on ordinary days, isn't it,
    when they happen,
those silent slippages,

a man mowing the lawn, a woman
    reading a magazine,
each thinking it can't go on like this,

then the raking, the turning
    of a page.
The art of letting pass

what must not be spoken, the art
    of tirade, explosion,
are the marital arts, and we,

their poor practitioners, are never
    more than apprentices.
At night in bed the day visits us,

happily or otherwise. In the morning
    the words good morning
have a history of tones; pray to say them

evenly. It's so easy, those moments
    when affection is what
the hand and voice naturally coordinate.

But it's that little invisible cloud
  in the living room,
floating like boredom, it's the odor

of disappointment mixing with
  kitchen smells,
which ask of us all that we have.

The man coming in now
  to the woman.
The woman going out to the man.

UPDATE

to Bartleby

There is the sky and here
is the grass, he said to you,
but you couldn't be fooled.
Not much has changed.
Nearby is the slavish city
and once upon a time
there was a God.
You'd be among our homeless,
nameless and cold.
The elms are dead, and fires
have taken acres of pines.
You'd never be able to tell
that the ocean has changed.
Here is the wind
and there are the balloons
the children have let go.
I know where I am, you said;
office, prison,
all the same to you.
There's the path
up the mountain where often
bear tracks have been seen,
and here the tree on which lovers
carved their names.
First they grew apart,
then they died.
The bears were interested
in berries. Like you,
they kept to themselves.

Love would have changed
everything for you,
but Melville was wise;
you'd have been forgettable,
bringing the costly bacon home.
The imagination still opens the door
we hesitate before,
still turns on the light.
Here is the book
in which you live
and here's what you've spawned:
drop-outs, slackards,
and a kind of dignity, a quaint
contagious way to refuse.
In the face of decency
how did you see the absurd?
The system still shows
its sweetest face, still sends out
an honest man with a smile.
Here are the foul-mouthed
gorgeous gulls,
and these are the walls
in which we live,
in which your heirs
call themselves free.
It's the end of the century;
almost everyone dreams of money
or revenge.

EVERYTHING ELSE IN THE WORLD

Too young to take pleasure
from those privileged glimpses
we're sometimes given after failure
or to see the hidden opportunity
in not getting what we want,
each day I subwayed into Manhattan

in my new, blue serge suit,
looking for work. College, I thought,
had whitened my collar, set me up,
but I'd majored in history.
What did I know about the world?

At interviews, if asked about the world,
I might have responded—citing Carlyle—
Great men make it go, I want to be one of those.
But they wanted someone entry-level,
pleased for a while to be small.

Others got the jobs;
no doubt, later in the day, the girls.
At Horn & Hardarts, for solace
at lunchtime, I'd make a sandwich emerge
from its cell of pristine glass.
It took just a nickel and a dime.

Nickels and dimes could make
a middleman disappear, easy as that,
no big deal, a life or two
destroyed, others improved.

But I wasn't afraid of capitalism.
All I wanted was a job like a book
so good I'd be finishing it
for the rest of my life.

Had my education failed me?
I felt a hankering for the sublime,
its dangerous subversions
of the daily grind.
Oh I took a dull, well-paying job.
History major? the interviewer said, I think
you might be good at designing brochures.

I was. Which filled me with desire
for almost everything else in the world.

NOT THE OCCULT

Because I was slow with girls
and didn't understand
they might like to be touched,
my girlfriend took my hand
and placed it on her breast.
We were sixteen. I just
left it there
as if I were memorizing,
which in fact I was.
It was all research and dream,
some fabulous connection
between my hand and her breathing,
then I was breathing like that too.

I've always been drawn
to such ordinary mysteries, women
and men, the broken bridge
between us. I like thinking
about night falling in a house
where anything can happen, and has,
strangers coming in
from their public outposts,
the drift of history
behind any wish to explain.
How to say what can't be said
across a table, or bed?

It's not the occult
and those obvious stakes
in the heart
that make me wonder.
And I confess

I have trouble speaking to people
fond of outer space.
I don't like riddles.
I'm tired of ambiguity's
old academic hush. Still ...

things happen,
and simply to record them
is often to deceive,
is even sometimes to mimic fog,
the way it's perfectly
yet inadequately clear about itself.

I'm thinking of that woman
returning from the restroom,
unable to recognize her husband.
She wasn't old, he hadn't disappeared,
though she perhaps had lost him.
Where is my husband? she asked the waiter,
who pointed toward the table.

And I'm thinking of the time
we lay ourselves down
among the dwarf pines,
looked up at the sky.
Nothing was new up there,
and down here the words for love
stuck in their history of abuse.
Angel, I wanted to say, meaning darling,
it seems heroic how we survive each other,
heroic that we try.

I'm thinking of the power of loveliness
to sadden.

Oh once there was such awe,
such a pure desire to praise.
There's not one of us
who inspires as much.

But I love the local and crude
somehow made beautiful, all the traces
of how it got that way erased.
And I love the corporeal body itself,
designed to fail,
and the mind, the helpless mind,
so often impelled to think about it.

12

TURNING FIFTY

I saw the baby possum stray too far
and the alert red fox claim it
on a dead run while the mother watched,
dumb, and oddly, still cute.
I saw this from my window
overlooking the lawn surrounded
by trees. It was one more thing
I couldn't do anything about,
though, truly, I didn't feel very much.
Had my wife been with me,
I might have said, "the poor possum,"
or just as easily,
"the amazing fox." In fact
I had no opinion about what I'd seen,
I just felt something dull
like a small door being shut,
a door to someone else's house.

That night, switching stations, I stopped
because a nurse had a beautiful smile
while she spoke about triage and death.
She was trying to tell us
what a day was like in Vietnam.
She talked about holding
a soldier's one remaining hand,
and doctors and nurses hugging
outside the operating room.
And then a story of a nineteen-year-old,
almost dead, whispering, "Come closer,
I just want to smell your hair."

When my wife came home late, tired,
I tried to tell her
about the possum and the fox,
and then about the young man
who wanted one last chaste sense
of a woman. But she was interested
in the mother possum,
what did it do, and if I did anything.
Then she wanted a drink, some music.
What could be more normal?
Yet I kept talking about it
as if I had something to say—
the dying boy
wanting the nurse to come closer,
and the nurse's smile as she spoke,
its pretty hint of pain,
the other expressions it concealed.

SIXTY

Because in my family the heart goes first
and hardly anybody makes it out of his fifties,
I think I'll stay up late with a few bandits
of my choice and resist good advice.
I'll invent a secret scroll lost by Egyptians
and reveal its contents: the directions
to your house, recipes for forgiveness.
History says my ventricles are stone alleys,
my heart itself a city with a terrorist
holed up in the mayor's office.
I'm in the mood to punctuate
only with that maker of promises, the colon:
next, next, next, it says, God bless it.
As García Lorca may have written: some people
forget to live as if a great arsenic lobster
could fall on their heads at any moment.
My sixtieth birthday is tomorrow.
Come, play poker with me,
I want to be taken to the cleaners.
I've had it with all stingy-hearted sons of bitches.
A heart is to be spent. As for me, I'll share
my mulcher with anyone who needs to mulch.
It's time to give up the search for the invisible.
On the best of days there's little more
than the faintest intimations. The millennium,
my dear, is sure to disappoint us.
I think I'll keep on describing things
to ensure that they really happened.

As the small plane descended through
the it's-all-over-now Sturm und Drang
I closed my eyes and saw myself
in waves of lucidity, a vanisher
in a long process of vanishing,
of solitary character, truant heart.
When we landed, I flipped down
my daily mask, resumed my normal
dreamy life of uncommitted crimes.
I held nothing against me anymore.
And now, next day, I wake before
the sound of traffic, amazed
that the paper has been delivered,
that the world is up and working.
A dazed rabbit sits in the dewy grass.
The clematis has no aspirations
as it climbs its trestle.
I pour myself orange juice, Homestyle.
I say the hell with low-fat cream cheese,
and slather the good stuff on my bagel.
The newspaper seems to be thinking
my thoughts: No Hope for Lost Men.
Link Between Laughter and Health.
It says scientists now know the neutrino
has mass. "The most ghostly particle
in the universe," one of them called it.
No doubt other scientists are jealous
who asked the right questions
too late, some small failure of intuition
leading them astray.

No doubt, too, at this very moment
a snake is sunning itself in Calcutta.
And somewhere a philosopher is erasing
"time's empty passing" because he's seen
a woman in a ravishing dress.
In a different hour he'll put it back.

WHAT THEY WANTED

They wanted me to tell the truth,
so I said I'd lived among them
for years, a spy,
but all that I wanted was love.
They said they couldn't love a spy.
Couldn't I tell them other truths?
I said I was emotionally bankrupt,
would turn any of them in for a kiss.
I told them how a kiss feels
when it's especially undeserved;
I thought they'd understand.
They wanted me to say I was sorry,
so I told them I was sorry.
They didn't like it that I laughed.
They asked what I'd seen them do,
and what I do with what I know.
I told them: find out who you are
before you die.
Tell us, they insisted, what you saw.
I saw the hawk kill a smaller bird.
I said life is one long leave-taking.
They wanted me to speak
like a journalist. I'll try, I said.
I told them I could depict the end
of the world, and my hand wouldn't tremble.
I said nothing's serious except destruction.
They wanted to help me then.
They wanted me to share with them,
that was the word they used, share.
I said it's bad taste
to want to agree with many people.

I told them I've tried to give
as often as I've betrayed.
They wanted to know my superiors,
to whom did I report?
I told them I accounted to no one,
that each of us is his own punishment.
If I love you, one of them cried out,
what would you give up?
There were others before you,
I wanted to say, and you'd be the one
before someone else. Everything, I said.

SUMMER NOCTURNE

Let us love this distance, since those who do not
love each other are not separated.
—SIMONE WEIL

Night without you, and the dog barking at the silence,
no doubt at what's *in* the silence,
a deer perhaps pruning the rhododendron
or that raccoon with its brilliant fingers
testing the garbage can lid by the shed.

Night I've chosen a book to help me think
about the long that's in longing, "the space across
which desire reaches." Night that finally needs music
to quiet the dog and whatever enormous animal
night itself is, appetite without limit.

Since I seem to want to be hurt a little,
it's Stan Getz and "It Never Entered My Mind,"
and to back him up Johnnie Walker Black
coming down now from the cabinet to sing
of its twelve lonely years in the dark.

Night of small revelations, night of odd comfort.
Starting to love this distance.
Starting to feel how present you are in it.

The new man unfolded a map and pointed
to a dark spot on it. "See, that's how
far away I feel all the time, right here,
among all of you," he said.

"Yes," John the gentle mule replied,
"alienation is clearly your happiness."
But the group leader interrupted,
"Now, now, let's hear him out,
let's try to be fair." The new man felt
the familiar comfort of everyone against him.

He went on about the stupidities
of love, life itself as one long foreclosure,
until another man said, "I was a hog,
a terrible hog, and now I'm a llama."
To which another added, "And me, I was a wolf.
Now children walk up to me, unafraid."

The group leader asked the new man,
"What kind of animal have you been?"
"A rat that wants to remain a rat," he said,
and the group began to soften
as they remembered their own early days,
the pain before the transformation.

ABOUT THE ELK AND THE COYOTES
THAT KILLED HER CALF

for Richard Selzer

The coyotes know it's just
    a matter of time,
but the elk will not let them

have her calf. You describe
    how they attack
and pull back, and how she goes on

repelling them, occasionally licking
    her calf's face,
until exhausted she turns

and gives it all up. So the elk,
    with her fierce
and futile resistance in which we

recognize something to admire,
    is held up
against the brilliant, wild

cunning of the coyotes.
    I love your sense
that the natural world stinks

and is beautiful and how important it is
    to have favorites.
Some part of us we'd like to believe

is essentially us, sides with the elk.
    Ah but tomorrow,
desperate, and night falling fast

and with a different sense of family . . .

AROUND THE TIME OF THE MOON

The experts were at work doing expert work.
Amateurs were loving what they hardly knew.
Houston, Tranquility Base here, the Eagle
has landed—came over our televisions,
accidental poetry, instant lore.
Our parents couldn't believe it.
Can you believe it? said my sister Sam.
Experts were being asked to explain themselves.
Agent Orange killed, but not before it burned.
A guy on acid said he was the bullet,
but sometimes also the wound.
The moon was finished, he went on to explain,
never again would haunt or beguile.
Mary Travers was leaving on a jet plane,
didn't know when she'd be back again;
I, for one, was sad. During the day
quotation marks descended from the sky,
fit around everything we thought we knew.
And under artificial light in our rooms,
we read strangely comforting books
about alienation and despair.
Soon everyone had a harmonica.
On every street corner, a guitar.
Many of us were love's amateurs,
its happy fools. The obstinate moon,
meanwhile, trod upon or not, kept bumping
up the crime rate, lifting the helpless seas.

DISCREPANCIES

It has something to do with ugliness,
even more, perhaps, with aggression,
but horseflies inspire no affection,
even though they're superb pilots.

Maybe because once they were squirmy,
furry things, butterflies seem content
with their sudden beauty, no interest
in getting anywhere fast.

The small brown bird outside my window
has a lilt and a tune. Elsewhere, a baby
is screeching. Watch out, little ones,
there are hawks, there are sleep-deprived

parents, utterly beside themselves.
When I was a child I claimed a grasshopper
hopped over a rock like a rockhopper.
"He likes to play with language," my mother

told her friends, "he's so smart."
She used to hide money in a coffee can,
place it behind the wooden matches
in the cupboard. I swear I never stole it.

She was beautiful, as was our neighbor
with the red jewel on her forehead.
That there's so little justice in the world—
one of them believed, the other experienced.

To ants a sparrow might as well be
a pterodactyl, and a parrot just one more
bright enormity to ignore
as they go about their business. I've tried

to become someone else for a while,
only to discover that he, too, was me.
I think I must learn to scrunch down
to the size of the smallest thing.

THE WIDENING

I was holding forth at the dinner table,
trying to fill what I perceived to be a void.
I had just read a book on music,
about which I know very little,
and, anticipating being corrected, was saying
something about the courage to have
a full stop, the courage to break off,
the breaking of rhythmic obligations.

Then the phone rang: my daughter's lost cat
had been found. I told everyone, and the void
seemed to fill a little with good cheer,
like vodka at the bottom of a glass.

So I told them that the baby crow
a hawk had tried to kill this morning
was still alive—three birds of different species
standing around it as if on guard.

The hawk was up on a nearby branch,
frowning, I said. No one smiled or laughed.

But we were mostly a dour group,
long neglected reciprocity dinners
finally acted upon, payback time,
and the social scientists among us—
who wouldn't know a good story
unless research confirmed it good—
wanted me to name the three species.
Flu-fly, plutark, Dickey-do—I couldn't
help myself—and the void widened again.

I wanted to go home, but I was home.

How about the hawk, my friend
Bjorn, the clarinetist, said,
and the hungers of the strong?
And by the way, he added,
there's no such thing as a full stop
in music—silence is a sound, an afterlife
for anyone with an ear.

I'd like to say I felt corrected, not betrayed,
and when I began to talk about miracles
and the Bee Gees singing "Stayin' Alive"
and Travolta being reborn before our eyes,
I'd like to say I didn't know why.

Actually, I did and didn't
want to say my mind had drifted
from music and obligations
to baseball, the beautiful choreography
of its dreams and errors. I wanted to say
that with some good stops at the right time
and some luck it's possible to survive.

I wanted to tell them that in my ignorance
I was serious, and that when things get lost
or are about to die all kinds of thoughts are legitimate.
It was my house, after all, and the floor was mine.

AFTERLIFE

There've been times I've thought worms
    might be beneficent, speeding up,
as they do, the dissolution of the body.

I've imagined myself streamlined, all bone
    and severity,
pure mind, free to contemplate the startling

absence of any useful metaphysics, any final
    punishment or reward.
Indulgences, not doubt. Romances I've allowed myself

when nothing ached, and the long diminishment
    seemed far off.
Today I want my body to keep making its sloppy

requests. I'm out among the wayward dazzle
    of the countryside,
which is its own afterlife, wild, repeatable.

There's no lesson in it for me. I just like
    its ignorant thrust,
it's sure way back, after months without desire.

Are wildflowers holy? Are weeds?
    There's infinite hope
if both are, but perhaps not for us.

To skirt the woods, to walk deeply like this
    into the high grass,
is to invoke the phantasms of sense

and importance. I think I'm smelling the rain
   we can smell before it rains.
It's the odor of another world, I'm convinced,

and means nothing, yet here it is, and here
   sweetly it comes
from the gray sky into the small openings.

13

DURING THE PANDEMIC

Many claimed for themselves
an understandable loneliness,
though for some it was a continuation
of a way of being, habitual,
tiresome, hard to befriend.

In the evenings, less lonely
by luck or circumstance,
I'd wet my soul
with wine, try to legitimize

who I was by vowing
not to nod to nonsense.
I was used to filling my life
with good cheer and the little
thrills of invention,

yet I heard how many lies
kept being repeated until
they sounded like the truth.
People were dying
and getting shot in the back

and knelt upon
until breathless. Suddenly
alone like never before
with the feelings of others
I understood

part of being excluded
is the need to claim as yours
everything
you can't expect
anyone will ever give you.

For my eulogist, in advance

Do not praise me for my exceptional serenity.
Can't you see I've turned away
from the large excitements,
and have accepted all the troubles?

Go down to the old cemetery; you'll see
there's nothing definitive to be said.
The dead once were all kinds—
boundary breakers and scalawags,
martyrs of the flesh, and so many
dumb bunnies of duty, unbearably nice.

I've been a little of each.

And, please, resist the temptation
of speaking about virtue.
The seldom-tempted are too fond
of that word, the small-
spirited, the unburdened.
Know that I've admired in others
only the fraught straining
to be good.

Adam's my man and Eve's not to blame.
He bit in; it made no sense to stop.

Still, for accuracy's sake you might say
I often stopped,
that I rarely went as far as I dreamed.

And since you know my hardships,
understand they're mere bump and setback
against history's horror.
Remind those seated, perhaps weeping,
how obscene it is
for some of us to complain.

Tell them I had second chances.
I knew joy.
I was burned by books early
and kept sidling up to the flame.

Tell them that at the end I had no need
for God, who'd become just a story
I once loved, one of many
with concealments and late-night rescues,
high sentence and pomp. The truth is

I learned to live without hope
as well as I could, almost happily,
in the despoiled and radiant now.

You who are one of them, say that I loved
my companions most of all.
In all sincerity, say that they provided
a better way to be alone.

1999

Hovering over the day:
staccato arcs and dashes
of marigold, mauve,
dark berry and lime
that seem to leap and converge.
No attempt here to resemble
or fool with nature,
but to catch hold of the feelings
I was left with after a stroll
through what now is a memory
of a stroll through a landscape
so dense I couldn't tell
green from greener.
The color of nightfall
is charcoal, and new words
are often needed, like verdancy
or the florescence of avocado
to help lighten, even separate
this mood I'm in from the mood
I'm trying to remember,
garish, yes, almost melancholy,
but still not fully named.

AN ABBREVIATED TOUR OF THE NOT YET FALLEN WORLD

The light would shine
then the night would fall,
and in those bedroom towns
outside cities
where many had gone
to escape the poor,
people I'd once been
and sometimes still am—
with investments and neuroses
and best intentions postponed—
would sleep a guarded sleep,
alert to the slightest sound.

The children would wake to daylight
they tended to ignore,
and all over our houses
screens would flicker
with new privacies, each to his own.
At work, I, too, rarely moved,
waiting at my machine
for the sudden to occur.
Even my disconnections
had a pleasing speed.

And when I wanted to move,
to literally fly,
the sky was forbidden
if I couldn't prove
I was my name.
Or, my license out, shoes off,
almost in the clear,

an agent might hold up
nail clippers, toothpaste,
want to know my secret plans.

I might then be asked to spread
my legs, extend my arms,
as if humiliation were a passage
to another world, and I'd be off
to some Houston or Atlanta,
a place they'd want me to agree
was my final destination.

Home would feel different
any time I'd reason to believe
I might not safely return.
Once, after circling in turbulence
then skidding on the runway,
living room took on new meaning.
I put my feet up on the ottoman,
and with a glass of Glenlivet
luxuriated in the company
of everything taken for granted.
Night wasn't falling, I could see it
slipping in through the trees,
rising from the marshes.
Nothing in it, I was sure,
contained a message.

Next morning, like every morning,
the dog moaned
about the same time sunlight
found a crack in the curtains.
No need for an alarm.
Juice and pastry and pills,
the newspaper open

first to yesterday's box scores
before any details
of our collective disgraces—

oh, how easy it is to control
how things begin.

I even saved the funnies for last,
as if such an order, because it was mine,
could possibly matter.

WHAT MEN WANT

Among the powerless,
unable to stop the ache that came
after someone else got the job
or the raise, my father just wanted
a little respect, some affirmation,
not always to be ruled
by the clock. My brother, too,

good man unequipped
to seize a day or leave a job
where everyone yelled,
brought the yelling home
the way others bring bread.
How else to make
his presence felt? And I,

in my chosen, happy torment
of words, spend entire days
cutting, stitching, rearranging,
trying to do what it takes
to be properly heard. Other days
I speak about books I love.
I feel like an escapee,
one big step ahead of my past.

Now I can afford to buy a ticket
to someplace else.
Now I can choose not to go.
Sometimes a man wants
because he discovers he can have.

No doubt this is why there are laws,
and why I'm grateful to my father
when I go too far
and covet, say, that Maserati
with its nifty slide-back roof
and five-on-the-floor.
My father who knew too well
what happiness isn't—his voice
inside me declaiming its clear No.

I wear his silver watchband,
a keepsake, for the sake of keeping.

What a man wants is to be rescued
from what he's not,
to test, then see what remains
of his inheritance.

And I'd like to think our hearts
are also in the business
of discovering their size,
and that another way to revise
is by adding on.

On weekends, my brother
would retreat to his garage,
desiring some honest praise
for fixing something broken.
Sometimes he'd want an evening out
with the boys, the indulgence
of shouting at an umpire,
or some merciless taking to task
of a slumping player.

After his stroke shocked
and rewired him, his anger left;
he never yelled again. Funny man
until the end, insistent hand holder,
at sixty-one he discovered
tenderness, witnessed the giving of it
come back to him.

No amount of justice or love
could have saved him, of course,
though just a little for a little while
must have felt like everything.

I want my list of everything
to include the approximate location
of the abyss, and its tolerance
for flirtation. I want no one
at the high stakes table
to intuit my pocket aces,
no one, any place, to suspect
that what I choose to reveal
is my way of withholding.

What a man wants is the power
to name the terms of his rescue,

and to know when it's time
to close the curtains,
usher in the private,
no longer live or resist
anyone else's story.

My father was a salesman
who meant every word he said,
though sometimes in a room
of strangers he'd shake
someone's hand too long,
or his smile would look
like a stuck, decided-on thing.

Just be yourself, he once counseled.
Who would want to know me then,
I thought, who would forgive me?

I've always needed paper and pencil
in order to speak as little as I should.
After the power to choose
a man wants the power to erase.

A POSTMORTEM GUIDE (2)

Once again for my eulogist,
in advance

You, too, are nineteen years older now,
and no doubt will say these roughly similar words
with a different sense of gravitas. I've changed,
but not as much as the world has.
I thought I had accepted all the troubles,
which is no longer true. And rage these days
has depleted that exceptional serenity
I once wanted you to claim I had.
Since you moved away we've hardly spoken,
and I'd understand if you feel you're now
the wrong man for the job. Back then
you were the only one who knew I had
an incurable disease. Well, no longer
can it be hidden. I stumble and fall,
shake and drool, but history's daily horror
trumps any condition of mine. What is it
compared to genocides and demagoguery?
There will be fewer people at the service this time,
perhaps a few grandchildren, maybe even a few
others who've read a few of my poems.
Tell them it was true, I *did* think I'd die at sixty,
in my prime, in love with mystery and its words.
What I wished for you to say was sincere. Then
I met a woman who chose to marry me, a man
unguaranteed, a selfish man who said he'd give her
five years. Tell them it was she who bargained
for ten, then fifteen, and is holding out for more.
Tell them everyone needs a persuasive advocate

to forestall the oncoming desolations of the heart.
If there are tears then, trust that you have broken
through to where thoughts of me have let loose
in them thoughts of opportunities they've missed,
a splendor unlived. Steady your voice, and tell them
even if we've known despair it's possible
with some luck and some love to wander,
sometimes happily, in the despoiled and radiant now.
End that way, because the whole truth,
as I've tried to say before,
is nothing anyone has to know.

2018

FINAL BOW

In my sleep last night
when the small world of everyone
who's mattered in my life
showed up to help me die,
I mustered the strength

to rise and bow to them—
a conductor's bow, that deep
bending at the waist, right arm
across my stomach,
the left behind my back.

At first it seemed like the comedy
of aging had revised an old scene—
how, with time running out,
I'd make the winning shot
in my schoolyard of dreams,

only now I was wearing
an unheroic hospital gown,
apparently willing to look foolish—
for what? what no longer mattered?—
before I lay again down.

INDEX OF TITLES AND FIRST LINES